Child Psychology & Adult Economics

Articles by: Jack C. Westman
James R. Walker
Deborah Walker

Commentary From:

Jay Belsky

Marian Blum

Richard Vedder

Robert Rector

Peter Barglow

Burton White

Maurice MacDonald

and others

Edited by Bryce Christensen

PUBLISHED BY THE ROCKFORD INSTITUTE

LIBRARY OF CONGRESS CATALOG CARD NUMBER

Christensen, Bryce J.

1989   89-63970

ISBN 0-9619364-2-8

Contents

The Rockford Institute

The purpose of The Rockford Institute is to rebuild an American ethical consensus rooted in the fundamental ideas and traditions of Western civilization. Through research, conferences, and publications, the Institute seeks to influence the moral and intellectual forces that shape social and cultural trends and public issues. The Institute has programs in the general areas of religion and society, the family, and literature. It is a non-profit, tax-exempt educational organization.

Publications

Chronicles: A Magazine of American Culture—A monthly magazine that considers the influence of ideas, arts, and letters upon the character and viability of American society.

The Family in America—In-depth analysis each month of a topic of long-range importance to the family and democratic capitalism; includes news and information.

The Religion & Society Report—A monthly newsletter surveying events, trends, and publications across the religious spectrum that influence American culture and public issues.

This World: A Journal of Religion and Public Life—A quarterly journal which provides in-depth analysis of religion and public issues.

Main Street Memorandum—A bimonthly newsletter of Institute achievements for contributors and friends, contains important Op-Ed placements.

Communication

Institute research is especially adapted for newspaper editorial pages. Materials have appeared recently in *The Wall Street Journal*, *USA Today*, *The Los Angeles Times*, *The Washington Post*, the *Chicago Tribune*, the *Chicago Sun-Times*, the *Houston Chronicle*, and numerous other newspapers throughout the country. Staff articles regularly appear in *The Public Interest*, *Commentary*, *Policy Review*, *Regulation*, *The American Spectator*, *Reason*, and other journals of scholarship and opinion. Talk show appearances by Institute staff include CBS *Nightly News*, NBC *News*, ABC's *Nightline*, William Buckley's *Firing Line*, CNN, CBN's *700 Club*, National Public Radio, and numerous local television and radio programs.

Administration

Allan C. Carlson, president of the Institute; Michael Y. Warder, executive vice president; Bryce J. Christensen, director of the Institute Center on the Family in America, editor of *The Family in America*; Thomas J. Fleming, editor of *Chronicles*; John A. Howard, counselor to the Institute and director of the Ingersoll program; and Harold O.J. Brown, director of The Center on Religion & Society, editor of *The Religion & Society Report*.

Board of Directors

Clyde Sluhan (Chairman), William Nelson (Vice Chairman), William Andrews, Allan Carlson, Clayton Gaylord, Mary Kohler, Robert Krieble, Norman P. McClelland, Dallin Oaks, George O'Neill, Jr., Henry Regnery, Robert Sandblom, James Bond Stockdale, Kathleen M. Sullivan, Katherine M. Swim, Frederick G. Wacker, Jr., Robert L. Woodson.

For more information:

Michael Warder, executive vice president; The Rockford Institute, 934 North Main Street, Rockford, Illinois 61103 (815) 964-5811.

Introduction

The current debate over day care has often degenerated into slogans and polemic. To shed light on this divisive issue, The Rockford Institute Center on the Family in America convened two consultations, one on December 6, 1988 on "The Risks of Day Care," attended by six leading child psychologists, and a second on "The Economics of Day Care" on April 21, 1989, attended by a more diverse group of economists and policy analysts from various backgrounds. By bringing together both the papers presented at these consultations and summaries of the ensuing discussions, this volume permits readers to see the underlying questions often obscured by headlines and rhetoric. Although recent actions in Washington have shifted the context for some of the comments made during the second consultation, the fundamental issues remain the same.

As the question perhaps most often neglected, the first consultation asked: How does day care affect children? Presenting the major paper at this consultation, Jack Westman, professor of psychiatry at The University of Wisconsin provided a sobering answer to this central question.

Against the claims made by day-care advocates, Dr. Westman concluded that "full-time day care, no matter how heavily funded, is not in the interests of young children, their parents, or society, because it is a response to the employment of parents . . . not to the needs of the children nor of the parents." "Children need the full range of spontaneous and intuitive interaction with adults who truly love them enough to sacrifice for them," he said, holding out little hope that day- care workers could provide such love.

Stressing the importance of "the attachment bonds of infants" to parents as "their emotional lifelines," Westman warned that day care often weakens such bonds. "The effect of interrupting attachment bonds during the first two years of life," he observed, "can be a failure to develop a basic trust in constant human relationships with other people." He especially worried about the long-term inter-generational effects of day care. He traced "the rancor, alienation, and strain of so many parent-child relationships" to inadequate parental devotion in a child's early years. Elderly parents, he predicted, would not receive loving attention from children neglected in their infancy.

Although some in attendance at the consultation complained that Professor Westman's judgments could not be empirically substantiated, most acknowledged the reality of troubling risks in day care. In the view of Burton White of the Parent Education Center, day care was so far from ideal that he strongly resisted the routine care of children by people outside the family. Because day care is implicated not only in emotional problems, but also in the spread of various childhood diseases (especially respiratory illnesses and middle-ear infections), White did not see much promise in the development of day-care centers, even if new government regulations were imposed.

For Professor Jay Belsky of Pennsylvania State University, day care poses the greatest risk for infants placed in full-time day care. He cited evidence showing that day care can cause such infants to avoid their own parents in a way that may be interpreted as disguised anger, "a false self." Such day-care children, he speculated, may develop "a manipulative type character." Looking at hints in the day-care research on insecurity, aggression, and noncompliance, Belsky conjectured that just possibly day care may be preparing children for a future in which everyone is out for himself more than ever before in the past.

Belsky admitted that because much of the evidence on day care is still fragmentary and inconclusive, it is still possible to deny any harmful effects. Yet he expressed surprise at the number of researchers who share his views on the risks of day care but who refuse to speak out. He also was dismayed that some colleagues have even urged him not to publish work likely to cause guilt among working mothers.

The social and ideological pressures on social scientists provoked spirited debate among those participating in the first consultation. White urged his colleagues to use their professional expertise as activists within the public debate. Belsky disagreed, fearing that the political pressures on the day-care debate might compromise the scientific objectivity of researchers. He cautioned that "social scientists . . . risk becoming the prostitutes of policymakers; we are slept with when there is desire and kicked out of bed when there is no longer interest." Belsky believed that while a bridge might be built between research findings and public policy, those crossing the bridge must clearly distinguish between the two. Professor Brian Vaughn of the University of Illinois at Chicago regarded the diversity of interest groups as a safeguard to scientific objectivity: No matter what empirical findings researchers report, they will find an interested audience.

Whatever political pressures social scientists may feel in doing research on day care, the pressures on the parents of young children are largely economic. Westman underscored the significance of these financial pressures in his paper. Vaughn stressed the economic loss to a household in which a mother drops out of the workforce in order to care for her children. But Belsky believed that many of the economic pressures on parents were self-imposed, a consequence of rising material expectations, not real need. He believed that Americans were devoting less attention to their children in part because they are obsessed with "the pursuit of materialistic goods." Aren't the smiles of children today, at this moment, valuable in their own right? Why doesn't that matter anymore? he asked.

The financial motivations of parents came under close scrutiny when The Rockford Institute Center on The Family in America convened a second consultation on "The Economics of Day Care." Although the first paper, presented by Professor James Walker, assistant professor of economics at The University of Wisconsin, was couched in the technical language of neoclassical economics, the formulae fit within broad cultural developments. In recent decades, married women have moved into the labor market in record numbers. Walker stressed that demand for day care is not *caused* by maternal employment; rather, the same forces which cause more young mothers to work also cause parents to place their children in day care. In part, Walker believed that changing employment and child-care patterns simply reflected shifting "tastes" or preferences among Americans. Between 1970 and 1985, married women with children under the age of three increased their participation in the labor market from just 25 percent to slightly over 50 percent. As possible reasons for this shift, Walker cited declining discrimination against female employment at a time when contraceptive technology has made it easier for women to plan their childbearing to accommodate educational and career aspirations. Working mothers find fewer options to day care because contemporary marriages fail so often and extended families are less available than in the past. Day care appeals to many women as the economic costs of not working have grown while government subsidy for day care has increased.

Deborah Walker, assistant professor of economics at Loyola University (New Orleans), took a close look in her paper at those pushing for greater government subsidy. Using a "public choice" framework, she revealed the rarely acknowledged economic motives of those advocating state subsidy for day-care child psychologists, day-care providers, state officials—all would benefit financially from increased government spending on day care. Walker especially noted the prominence of these groups in the recent movement for the ABC Bill for expanding Federal support for day care.

As participants responded to the papers by the two Professor Walkers (not related!), not all agreed about the importance of economics in driving up demand for day care. The evidence appeared mixed to Robert Rector of The Heritage Foundation. Three-quarters of all mothers still state that they would prefer to remain at home with their children when finances permit. But on the other hand, the real income of single-earner households— adjusted for inflation—has actually risen since the 1950's. Husbands in two-earner households do not earn significantly less on average than husbands in one-earner households. Something other than economics alone must be driving the move toward day care.

Allan Carlson thought that the move toward day-care could fit within a broad historical surrender by the household of its economic functions to the marketplace, a trend presciently foreseen by Charlotte Perkins Gilman. Even cleaning and food preparation now are increasingly handled more efficiently outside the home. The rise of day care signals the home's loss of its last significant economic function. Despite this trend, however, Carlson stressed the significant residual value of the work of a mother who stays home. Because of this home production, mothers may still find it to their financial advantage to stay at home— so long as government policy doesn't skew the incentives.

For Maurice MacDonald, professor of family economics at The University of Wisconsin, government policy could prove decisive in determining how completely the marketplace displaces the family. Others seconded this judgment. Richard Vedder, professor of economics at Ohio University, noted that if taxes and welfare assistance are taken into account, the economic status of the single-earner family has deteriorated in recent years.

Past and proposed policies on day care have not favored the interests of one-earner households. Again and again, Rector deplored the indifference, if not outright hostility of Washington policymakers toward the traditional family. Traditional families are far more numerous than those policymakers will admit, but their needs are rarely taken into account. Past tax credits for day care have benefitted two- earner households at the expense of traditional households. The proposed ABC Bill would exacerbate this injustice, forcing low-income traditional families to subsidize day care for two-earner households enjoying much higher income. But because they are poorly organized, traditional families exert little pressure in Congress. Vedder went even further in condemning the antifamily effects of government policy. Because children do not vote, government may be "inherently anti-child," he ventured.

Nor do traditional families fit within the ideologies that motivate many politicians. Traditional families must react to cultural pressures broader than politics. Vedder suggested that Americans today simply don't like children as much as they used to, enumerating a number of developments—teen suicide, failing schools, child poverty—that reflect a declining interest in children. For Stephen Chapman of *The Chicago Tribune*, the recent retreat from childbearing fits within a pattern stretching back for two centuries. As their affluence has risen, Americans have borne fewer and fewer children. It is the anomaly of the "baby boom" which requires explanation, in Chapman's view.

Speaking for the traditional homemaker, Judith Finn lamented that "kids really aren't the central concern" for an increasing number of American women. "Our whole understanding of what it is to raise a child has changed," she declared. Finn did not stand alone in emphasizing the importance of changing cultural attitudes toward maternal child-rearing. At the second consultation, Vedder and Rector both spoke against the new cultural bias against the homemaker. Belsky and Westman sounded the same theme in the first consultation. The at-home mother has become "a voiceless soul" (Belsky's term) in contemporary America, consigned to the same cultural limbo as the working mother of the 1950's.

As a participant in both consultations, I evaluate both events by posing again Leo Tolsoy's famous question: What do men (and women) live by? For those who live by their hopes for a statist utopia, day care is a step forward in the move of social progress. Collective child care, after all appears as a standard feature of utopian literature from Plato to B.F. Skinner. For those who live by the creeds of self-fulfillment or material advancement, day care constitutes an agreeable modern convenience. For the millions who live merely by conformity to prevailing trends—they know not why—day care represents just one more fashion to be accepted, like the modes of home furnishing or skirt length. For a significant minority of hard- pressed Americans—especially divorced mothers—who live by the skin of their teeth, day care counts as a grim necessity. On the other hand, for those who live by cherishing bonds of memory and love between the generations, day care appears as a troubling innovation, a threat to the links between generations. For those who see their family commitments as part of their devotion to God, day care may be regarded as a devilish snare, a spiritual trap for parents and children.

Even among those who live to bear witness to the human spirit rather than to divine grace, day care may appear deeply suspect. Two of the greatest writers of this century—Aldous Huxley and Yevgeny Zamyatin—have depicted collectivized child care as part of a dehumanizing future. The main character in Zamyatin's *We* is cared for in a "child-rearing factory" but as an adult yearns for a mother who will regard him not as a number but as "a simple human being—a piece of herself."

The debate over childcare will continue, as it should, over empirical, psychological, and economic questions. I hope this book helps to clarify that debate. But as the evidence is sorted out and the various policies are assessed, the deepest line of cleavage will reflect diverging commitments of the heart.

— *Bryce J. Christensen*
Rockford Illinois
May 1989

The Risks of Day Care For Children, Parents, and Society

by Jack C. Westman, M.D.

In the past, America's children have come to public attention only when something goes wrong in their lives. When they were over-worked, we instituted child labor laws. When they created problems on the streets in our growing cities, we instituted public education. When they appeared in hospitals as battered children, we devised programs for child abuse and neglect. When they are not as well educated as foreign children, we devote more attention to public education. For the first time in history, we now are concerned about what kind of care is best for them.

More specifically, the quality of care young children receive while their parents are employed away from home has become an important social issue. For young children, there are three kinds of non-parental day care in the United States, according to U.S. Census Bureau data for 1984-1985 (U.S. Bureau of the Census, 1987). The term day care is more accurate than child care, because it is defined and necessitated by the hours of the day during which employed parents are unavailable to their children. The most common form of day care is "family" or "home-based" care which 37 percent of the children of employed parents receive in homes other than their own. The second is "sitter" care in the child's home for 31 percent. The third is "institutional" care in school-like centers for 23 percent.

Because of its especially controversial nature, institutional day care for infants and toddlers is the particular focus of this paper. The issues posed by very young children differ from those posed by 3 and 4 year olds. In order to present the perspectives of children, parents, and society, I will touch on the meaning of children to parents in the United States, the impact of full-time parental employment on fami-lies, the day-care constituencies, the effects of day care on children, the developmental needs of infants and toddlers, day-care and public policies, and society's stake in child care.

There are two fundamental issues. The first is whether parents and children should continue to be required to adjust to adult-oriented workplaces traditionally dominated by men with homemak-ing wives, or whether workplaces should adjust to families in which both men and women bear child-rearing responsibilities. The second is whether government should increase its role in the institutional care of children or support families as child-rearing units.

As with abortion, the death penalty, and other controversial social issues, the debate about day care has become emotionally polarized. At its roots are beliefs about morality and the role of government in private life, colored by racism, sexism, and ageism. In addition, the nonparental care of children ignites the latent conflict between the world of the family and the world of employment. For some, it symbolizes an assault on traditional family values; they resist reforms in day care that could improve the lives of millions of children. For others, it enables women to compete in traditional workplaces; they resist acknowledging the disadvantages of day care, as do the providers of day care.

The Meaning of Children to Parents in the United States

The present situation cannot be fully understood without an appreciation of the evolution of parent-child relationships in this country. The styles of parenting in any society vary widely under the influence of cultural and social conventions. In the United States, the contemporary variety of parenting arrangements and apparent dispersion of families has obscured the fact that there has been a gradual evolution of parenting toward more intimate, egalitarian relationships between parents and children.

The past historic gap between the generations has resulted from tentative, ambivalent, and even distant relationships between parents and children (Westman, 1979). Until the advent of sanitation and modern medicine, the high rate of infant and childhood mortality discouraged parental emotional investment in offspring who might not survive at all. Moreover, the wealthy often have delegated parenting to governesses; the poor have relied upon children as sources of income and security in old age; and the inhibition of emotional expressiveness has limited intimate relationships between middle-class parents and their children.

Over the last century in the United States, children have been progressively recognized as developing human beings by child labor and education laws. More recently, the legal rights of children have been recognized. Now attention is being paid to their developmental needs. As children have become less economic assets and more financial burdens, their value to adults has been stripped to its psychological and affectional core. The motivation of contemporary parents to have and rear children is largely based on love and the potential of lifelong friendships with them. Children are psychological extensions and sources of purpose in life for parents. This is painfully apparent in the bitterness of child-custody disputes resulting from parental divorces.

The signs of intimacy between parents and children are evident in extreme situations in which some parents obtain sexual satisfaction from their children. Others depend upon their children as quasi-adult companions, and many adulate their children. More typically, parents are sensitive to the developmental needs of their children as reflected in the widespread concern about the care of young children. Many mothers and fathers feel worried and guilty about the available options for placing their children in the care of other people during full-time working hours. As a result, many parents are weighing the priorities of caring for their young children, their careers, and their financial expectations.

On the other hand, parents are heavily involved in the development of their careers and dependent upon income levels generated by full-time employment. For many of them, sacrifices are made in their family lives in order to accommodate to their conditions of employment. Unfortunately, these employed parents fail to recognize the power that could be generated from their vast numbers in the work force and from their critical importance to the functioning of most businesses. They have not fully linked their working conditions and benefits to their responsibilities as parents, in part because adults without dependents often are regarded as ideal employees. Consequently, parents may be reluctant to admit that family concerns interfere with their work performance. Fathers especially may hesitate to speak out for family benefits, because doing so does not fit with a competitive, masculine image.

The Impact of Full-Time Parental Employment on Family Life

Because of the full-time employment of their parents, many young children are experiencing a completely different world from the one in which their parents were raised. Numerous caregivers in homes and institutions, such as nursery schools and day-care centers, now share child rearing with parents and other relatives. The lifestyle that necessitates day care is depicted by the following family (Webb, 1984):

The Armstrongs are what used to be called a typical American family, consisting of a mother, a father, and two children: a four-year-old boy, Adam, and a six-year-old girl, Eve.

One January morning the alarm goes off at 5:30 a.m. Mrs. Armstrong gets up quietly, dresses in the dark, resets the alarm for 6:30 a.m. and goes downstairs. There she makes coffee, sets the table for four, and then sits down and eats breakfast alone. She leaves the house by 6:15 a.m. to get to the hospital by 6:45 a.m., where she works as a nurse on the 7:00 to 3:00 p.m. shift.

At 6:30 a.m. the alarm goes off again and Mr. Armstrong gets up, wakes Adam and Eve, and begins getting dressed. Adam brushes his teeth and watches his father shave, while Eve tries to get her father's attention by asking him which of the two new toys she received for her birthday she should take to school for Show and Tell. Mr. Armstrong suggests that she take one today and one tomorrow, and then he tells both children to hurry and finish dressing. He follows Eve into her room where he brushes her hair and lets her choose which color barrette she wants to wear.

After cereal and milk, the father and children leave the house together around 7:30 a.m. Eve kisses her father goodbye and walks alone to a house down the street where she goes in the back door and waits with her friend, Rachel, until 8:15 a.m., when it is time for them to leave for school together. Eve will return to Rachel's house after school and remain there until her mother picks her up sometime between 3:45 p.m. and 4:30 p.m. (depending on how many errands Mrs. Armstrong has to do after work).

Meanwhile, Mr. Armstrong and Adam drive to the day-care center where Mr. Armstrong parks the car and accompanies his son into the building. After helping Adam off with his jacket, Mr. Armstrong begins his daily 45 minute drive to his job in the city. It is 8:00 a.m., and the road is crowded as usual with other commuters.

Adam spends eight hours per day, five days per week at the day-care center, where approximately half of the 14 children in his group have been his classmates for over one year. Adam's 40-hour week in day care equals the time his parents spend at their jobs. On Saturdays, Adam goes with his sister to his maternal grandparents for the day, while his mother attends Saturday college, and his father works on a second job in his father-in-law's business. Mrs. Armstrong is studying for an additional nursing degree. The parents want to buy their own home and are trying to save for the down payment.

The children's time with their parents is limited to one hour alone with their father in the morning five days a week; approximately three hours per day alone with their mother (in the late afternoon from 4:00 p.m. to 7:00 p.m.) and one-and-a-half to two hours per day with both parents together before bedtime. On Saturday, Adam and Eve play with their cousins at the grandparents' house. They see no more of their parents on Saturdays than on regular week-days, but on Sunday the family spends most of the day together, occupied with never-ending routine household chores interspersed with deliberate attempts on both parents' parts to spend some time individually with each child.

As this illustration demonstrates vividly, family life is diluted by the busy lives of contemporary parents and their increasing use of full-time day care for young children. Most parents realize that the decision to put their child in someone else's care, and the choice as to the kind of arrangement, significantly affects their own lives. But few are aware of how full-time day care affects their children. Moreover, the impact of the extensive use of full-time day care on the nature and direction of our society is not fully appreciated.

Many employed parents would prefer to care for their own babies and toddlers. They find that their emotional bonds with their children are overridden and diluted by separation during their hours of employment, often eight to twelve hours a day, five days a week. The situation is particularly serious for parents who must work to barely sustain a livelihood and who only can afford child care of questionable quality. This is a much greater problem for women than for men.

There are two categories of women who have to work. One consists of women without husbands and the other of women whose husbands earn too little to support a desired standard of living. Forty-five percent of all working women are without husbands, and two-thirds of all single-parent mothers work. For women with husbands, however, the statistical evidence is that wives are almost as likely to work when their husbands earn $35,000 as when they earn less than $25,000 a year (Fallows, 1985, p. 139). The perception of having to work, therefore, varies considerably and often depends less on straightforward economic pressures than on personal and societal definitions of success, self-fulfillment, family obligations, and material desires.

Many families decide that the financial costs of forgoing a second income or settling for a part-time income are easier to bear than the emotional costs of trying to earn two incomes (Davidson, 1988). This is suggested by the fact that thirty-four percent of mothers of children under the age of three are employed only part-time. Thus, nearly two-thirds of the mothers of infants and toddlers do not work away from home or have part-time jobs. A full-time homemaker explained (Ward, 1988):

> For me, being a homemaker is akin to being a college student. I'm learning skills and enhancing relationships that will be important for the rest of my life. I'm devoting a relatively small number of years creating what I hope will be strong bonds with my daughter and husband and without the pressure that can build in a two-career family. I see it as a stage of life rather than a lifetime career.

In the light of these complexities, it is no wonder that day care is an emotional topic that tends to polarize people as a political issue. Some maintain that without it, young families who need two incomes to manage and single parents cannot survive. Others believe that the large numbers of women in the work force contribute to the high cost of living that now necessitates two breadwinners to support a family in contrast with one in the past. Still others seek unionization of day-care workers in order to improve their low salaries.

Day-care advocates see day care as essential for women, if they are to fulfill themselves psychologically and if they are to achieve their rightful place in society. They see day care as a positive influence on the social and cognitive development of children and as an antidote to the psychiatric problems seen in family-reared children. However, its critics see day care as an abdication of the parental role by a narcissistic generation of adults. They see it as undermining the family and as a socialistic way to raise children. Some see it as a fulfillment of George Orwell's *1984* world in which the family is replaced by child-rearing institutions with the loss of enduring personal relationships. These biases and the perspectives of the day-care constituencies obscure examination of day care from the point of view of the affected children.

The Day-Care Constituencies

The advocates of institutional day care represent three constituencies: 1) employed parents, 2) day-care child-development specialists, and 3) the day-care system itself. Notably absent is a constituency representing the interests of children.

(1) *Employed Parents*

The mechanization of housekeeping tasks after World War II, combined with the growing use of birth control, contributed to the availability of women for the work force. Further encouraged by the advocacy of the rights of women following the Civil Rights Act of 1964, the momentum for the employment of women was accelerated by the economic inflation of the 1970's. The resulting decrease in family purchasing power forced many women to find jobs in order to maintain their previous standard of living. At the same time, the growth in the service economy created new opportunities for employment for them.

Inherent in the pressure from parents for day care are beliefs and values related to gender roles and the existential value of children. More specifically, attitudes about motherhood and about child-rearing reflect the prevailing social values of a particular era. For example, an 1898 publication titled *Ideal Motherhood* warned mothers about relinquishing the care of their children to "hirelings" (Davis, 1898):

> The children's nurses in stately homes are sometimes more truly the mothers of the little ones they watch and tend more than the women who love them. The woman who delegates the entire care of her children to hirelings, no matter how wisely chosen, misses the best that can be given to her and sells her divine birthright of motherhood for empty glitter and excitement.

The song of a sweatshop-working father, written in 1887, reveals the anguish parents can feel when the need to work takes them away from their children. That father described his pain at being a stranger to his own child:

> I have a handsome baby son,
> A little boy so fine.

And when I look at him, I feel
The whole world is mine.

But seldom do I see my child
When he's awake and bright.
When I leave home, he's still asleep,
When I return, it's night.

I look at him in anguish then,
I know it seems so clear—
When once again my child awakes—
His Daddy won't be here.

—Translated by Ruth Rubin

By 1970, popular views about child rearing had changed so completely that social historian Philip Slater (1970) felt compelled to expose what he termed "the magnification of motherhood" among post-World War II middle class American housewives. He was critical of the views expressed by Anna Freud, Leon Yarrow, and Selma Fraiberg, among many others, that singled out the mother-child relationship as the unique prototype of all later love relationships (Webb, 1984).

In contrast, John Bowlby's writings about attachment (1969, 1973, & 1980) added more scientific fuel to the conviction that the mother's role was crucial for the healthy development of the young child. Although Bowlby's theory of attachment was based on the belief that a child's tendency to attach was instinctual and served the purpose of survival, the psychoanalytic and social-learning view was that the child becomes attached to the ministering person because of need satisfaction and the reinforcement of pleasure. The end result of both positions was the same: establishment of the exquisite and near exclusive importance of the mother-child relationship in human development as an axiom. In this view, a child's attachment to the mother is diluted, or compromised, by competing, and possibly numerous, attachments to other caregivers.

At the same time, Margaret Mead advanced the idea that concepts of gender are principally cultural, not biological. Implicit in this new definition of gender was rejection of the idea that "biological destiny," deriving principally from sexual differences, is at work in human affairs. This helped revive feminism as a national movement.

The feminist wave in the United States during the early years of this century made significant headway but lost momentum during the conservative 1920's and the depression-ridden 1930's. Then and now, women bear the major responsibility for child care and household management, leading to difficulty in competing with their male colleagues. From this point of view, modern feminism has called for a revolution in child rearing, so that women will be able to excel in their careers (Graubard, 1987).

All of this has contributed to the contemporary ideological shift toward equalization of male and female roles in our society (Gordon, 1988). Still, the conflicts between employment and child-rearing often are no-win situations for many women. Mothers of the 1950's who entered the work force were made to feel guilty and negligent. Since the 1970's, women who are not employed away from home are made to feel incomplete.

Parents face conflicting peer group and societal pressures as the traditional roles of mothers and fathers are changing. Mothers are criticized by some feminists if they prefer to raise their own children, because women are needed in the work force so that our nation can take full advantage of its resources. These feminists have de-emphasized the uniqueness of mothers in order to promote equal participation of fathers and mothers in child-rearing. On the other hand, although less than in the past, men still may be criticized by their employers and peers, if they want to take a more active role in raising their children. More commonly, men are unwilling to share child-rearing responsibilities. Both men and women are imbued with the social value that only remunerative work is worthwhile and personally fulfilling. Domestic work is seen as part of private life and without financial value. The homemaker is treated as a consumer but not as a productive worker. For this reason, the limitation of the term "working parents" to those who are employed away from home contributes to the denigration of the financial worth of the work of parenting (Bose et al., 1987).

In our society, the general view that mothers have the primary responsibility for providing child care has not changed substantially with the return of many mothers to the work force. One of the most important barriers to thinking clearly about the developmental needs of children is the resentment borne by many women, because they are expected to make greater sacrifices in their lives for their children than are their husbands. The split between family life and employment allows men to ignore the problem of caring for children. Children are lumped into the family sphere. Furthermore, men have not experienced the interferences with their careers caused by the "buck-stops-here" responsibility of women for children (Pogrebin, 1983, p. 135).

The entry of many women into the paid work force reflects the special obstacles young families must overcome to hold onto the middle-class living standard taken for granted by their parents (Levy, 1988). The social acceptability of divorce also has played a role in increasing the cost of living by creating separate households after divorce. More fundamentally, the loss of purchasing power of the still-inflated dollar has forced women to join the paid work force in order to maintain family life styles. For example, between 1947 and 1973, the average worker's inflation-adjusted earnings rose sixty-one percent. Since 1973, however, the average inflation-adjusted earnings have fallen fifteen percent, reflecting a decrease in national purchasing power.

Women are attracted to employment away from home for a variety of reasons beyond financial: professional and intellectual stimulation, escape from perceived tedium and boredom, peer and collegial associations, challenges for greater self-fulfillment and self-development, and a desire for economic independence from their husbands (Physician Survey, 1985). In addition are several frequently overlooked underlying psychological factors.

The first, for some parents, is the overwhelming challenge for creativity that rearing young children involves. They are attracted to the structure and predictability of work routines as less troublesome than the responsibilities for decision-making and the leadership of child-rearing. They prefer the sense of achievement that comes from self-limited projects with tangible outcomes. Although there are household tasks that can be completed, they do not provide the kind of satisfaction for these parents that comes from earning money or accomplishing objectives at the workplace.

A second factor for some parents is an aversion to the emotional intensity of interacting with young children. For them, the workplace is an attractive haven of relative tranquility. Many mothers wonder if they are cut out to be parents and are attracted by the promotion of day care as desirable for the development of their children. They can relieve themselves of the burdens of child-rearing with the belief that they are helping their child. Clinical experience suggests that a major factor behind the delegation of child care by parents who question their own child-rearing abilities is a lack of modeling of harmonious and competent parenting during their own childhoods. Moreover, many parents have experienced discordant family lives including abuse, molestation, and parental divorce. Their past negative experiences in families and hesitancy in forming intimate relationships affects their relations with other adults, their own spouses, and their children and leads them to avoid the discomfort they experience at home with their children.

The third factor is a desire for adult companionship. The home environment lacks ready access to other adults, and alternative ways of obtaining it are more difficult to explore than is obtaining a job.

For mothers, there are three points at which the question of employment away from home arises: at the end of their maternity leaves, when their children are ready for nursery school at the age of three, and when the youngest child enters the first grade. Influencing their decisions are the expectation that they will return to the work force as soon as possible, as if childbirth were merely an illness and physical recovery was all that mattered.

In general, the movement of women into the labor force has created a social revolution in its own right. Two out of every three new labor market entrants since 1975 have been women. The employment rate for women with children under 18 years of age has grown from 46 percent in 1975 to 55 percent in 1986. For women with children under the age of three, it has increased from 34 percent to 51 percent, including both the part- and full-time employed, over this same time span. This dramatic change in the labor market was completely unpredicted by demographers and forecasters (Briggs, 1987). The resulting need for day care has sorely overtaxed available facilities with resulting stress for parents, children, employers, and society.

The current generation of parents of young children have less time to spend with their children and higher achievement anxiety in relation to themselves and their offspring. With good intentions, they leave their children with different caretakers over the early years of the child's life (Gallagher & Coche, 1987). The illusion of affluence places them in the position, previously reserved for the wealthy, of hiring others to do what are deemed the menial chores of child care. Narcissistic parents can use prestigious day care to display their material devotion to their children. Their question is how little time can be spent with infants and toddlers without harming them; not what is best for their children. Behind this question lies the commonly held belief in our society that there are more important things for adults to do than spend time with children. Parenthood often is demeaned. The wealthy hire caretakers for their children, and the status of those who care for them is low. As a result, the social pressure on parents is to value time spent in remunerative employment more than in parenting. There is little recognition of the pleasures and satisfactions of parenting. Still for most employed parents, their families are the most important source of emotional support (Kamerman, 1980, p. 135). They seek reassurance that their children, well or sick, are being lovingly cared for while they are working.

(2) Day-Care Child-Development Specialists

Support for day care as a positive influence for children and society is advanced by those child-development professionals who feel that young children in day care benefit from multiple relationships and education.

Beatrice Whiting (1963) pointed out that American culture ranks far above other societies in the importance placed on the mother's presence at home with the children all or most of the time. In 1954, Margaret Mead suggested that cross-cultural studies show that adjustment is most facilitated if a child is cared for by many warm, friendly people. In 1962, Mead further argued that children with multiple caretakers may actually be better off than the child involved in a mother-child pair relationship which, because of its exclusivity, predisposes the child to trauma when this key relationship is disturbed by separation.

For those who question the benefit of day care for infants, the point has been made that the effects of day care on the infants themselves is not the most important issue (Cummings & Beagles-Ross, 1984).

> The present research highlights the need for researchers to be more sophisticated in their consideration of day care as a problem for research. The issue is not simply a polemic: to prove day care is good or bad for infants. This view is useless from a social policy perspective; the need for out-of-home care for infants will continue to be an inevitable byproduct of changes in economic conditions and parents' roles.

In another vein, the points are made to employers that day care is in their interests to protect their investments in the present, as well as the future, work force and that day care improves parents' performance on the job (Galinsky, 1986). Public policymakers also are informed that the future taxpayers of America will pay more taxes if they learn as children in day care that it is appropriate to work well (Gunzenhauser & Caldwell, 1987, p. 113).

Ellen Galinsky and Diane Hughes of Bank Street College in New York, found that child-care problems negatively affected work performance in a study carried out for *Fortune Magazine* in 1987. Because of the high turnover rate of child-care workers (40 percent for centers and 62 percent for in-home care), difficulties in finding child care contributed to lowered productivity, symptoms of stress, and absenteeism of parents. Of interest is the parents' perception of the problem: 16 percent of the men and 21 percent of the women felt that their families interfered with their jobs; whereas 37 percent of the men and 41 percent of the women felt that their jobs interfered with their family lives. As a result, one in four workers reported taking a less demanding job or refusing promotion because of family considerations.

The day care of young children has grown from informally arranged child-care arrangements to becoming a commercial industry, a professional field, and a movement with a political constituency of its own. In addition to day-care providers, a bureaucracy has grown in order to administer regulations, monitor programs, and serve parents.

The national state of child-care regulations was surveyed in 1986 (Morgan, 1987). It revealed that 41 states have updated their requirements in the last five years, but they fall behind current knowledge. For example, 26 states have no regulations regarding group size for infants and toddlers. In order to improve the day-care field, child-care workers are trying to assume professional status with training requirements, facility standards, training programs, research undertakings, and licensing procedures. Two obvious reasons for this professionalization are to improve the salaries of day-care workers in order to attract and hold competent people and to improve the quality of the care. This means that a growing number of people depend upon day care for their livelihoods. An indication of the boundaries of the day-care "turf" was reflected in Sandra Scarr's expressed concern that physicians and clinical child psychologists are encroaching inappropriately on the field of child care by commenting on day care (Gunzenhauser & Caldwell, 1987, p. 136).

3) *The Day-Care Industry*

Commercial day-care providers are concerned about marketing their services and are attempting to overcome their image as "babysitters" by stressing the benefits of their offerings (ibid., p. 165). The first benefit is quality child care as measured by professional standards and provided by professional caregivers. A second related benefit is that children will receive the advantages of child-development research and technologies. A third benefit is that the lack of experience and compromised coping abilities of immature and marginally competent parents can be remedied by the educational and treatment services of day-care facilities.

Because of the institutional nature of their services, day-care providers have their own needs and dynamics that can compete or conflict with a family's. This can result in an attitude on the part of the day-care staff that the emotional reactions of the children and their parents are problems to be resolved rather than legitimate expressions of pain and loss (Cummings & Beagles-Ross, 1984). This is exemplified by the following excerpt from an infant day-care manual (Rositer, 1982):

> . . . parental feelings of jealousy and anger are most intense, especially for a first-time parent taking the baby to an experienced caregiver. Recognizing the potential for problems and openly discussing them with the day-care staff are the first steps toward their resolution. There is a point where parents can learn from the caregiver; there also is a point where parents must assert their judgment and desires—even if they are seen as "wrong" by the day-care staff.

The trend toward viewing day care as a professional activity places caregivers in roles with educational and therapeutic elements. In addition to helping, this can create a distance between caregiver and parent. The fact that this has occurred and that there is a need for someone to mediate between day-care staff members and parents is reflected in the statement by Ellen Galinsky: "We should work toward having parent advocates in child care settings . . . to take the parents' perspective" (ibid., p. 68). The intrinsic tension between parents and caregivers is compounded by the fatigue of parents and the low income and status of day-care employees. As an example, stressed parents who feel their children are unhappy at their place of care often blame the particular program and switch centers. Day-care centers, in turn, are sensitive to the financial impact of the withdrawal of children and, therefore, may not report children's distress to their parents.

A day-care center oriented to the developmental needs of children would have a staff-to-child ratio larger than what is commonly recommended or required (Blum, 1983). It would have spacious, sunny facilities; good, well maintained indoor and outdoor equipment; plentiful supplies; nutritious and attractive food; adequate funds for janitorial services and sanitation; and health services. It would have several well-paid caregivers with each small group of children, so that there would always be adequate care and so that the teachers could take needed sick leaves and vacations without impairing the functioning of the group or the sense of security of any individual child. There would be separate areas for play, for eating, for sleeping, and for isolation during minor illnesses. Because the staff would be paid well and the workload would be manageable, there would be little staff turnover, so that a young child could have the same caregivers over time. There would be enough funds to provide for frequent staff meetings and for in-service staff training. There would be adequate funds for consultation with social workers, clinical psychologists, and nutritionists and for the implementation of a supportive parent program. Unfortunately, such a center would be economically infeasible. Much less than this is accepted as quality day care at costs of over $130 a week:

> The median annual wage of a full-time woman worker is about $16,200. Rita Watson of the Yale University Bush Center estimates the cost of adequate quality child care—requiring more, better-paid and better-trained staff—at $7,800 a year for infants and $6,500 for toddlers. These expenses, plus taxes and work costs, would often eliminate most of the extra income from a second job (Samuelson, 1988).

As is evident, day care involves complexities, ambiguities, and ironies caused by the conflicting needs and goals of each of its constituencies. Tradeoffs to resolve those conflicts are usually at the expense of the other constituencies. Notable by its complete lack of representation is the most important constituency of all—the children.

The Effects of Day Care on Children

The director of Madison, Wisconsin's Community Service Division said that she fears we are involved in a huge social experiment in which we take middle-class children and subject them to the same social problems only disadvantaged children experienced ten years ago: overcrowding, lack of planning, lack of stimulation, and lack of adult attention (Conniff, 1988). One day-care worker described the experience of the children as follows:

> For ten hours a day, these kids have to interact with 20 or
> 30 other kids. They find it hard to keep going as they head
> into the final stretch each afternoon.
>   Imagine if we adults had to constantly be trying to get
> along with that many people. And then some parents come
> expecting to take their kids to gymnastics or some other les-
> son. And they wonder why the child is crying. It can all be
> too much (Hume, 1988).

Numerous studies of the effects of day care on parents and children report both that it does and does not harm children. In fact, the usual research techniques cannot answer this question. The traditional view of science has undergone radical revision. The empirical accumulation of facts without a theoretical basis has been discarded by the physical sciences but remains the approach of the behavioral sciences (Kuhn, 1977). Most importantly, the inherent bias of observers is taken for granted, as is the influence of the observer in the phenomena observed. Consequently, no single study can be taken out of context of the subject's life and the researcher's bias.

The research questions about the effects of early day care revolve around emotional health, personality development, and family relationships. We do know that early parent-child attachments are important factors in each of these areas, for impairments are found in them with gross disruptions or failures in child-parent attachments. However, the effects of moderate and mild alterations would not be known for years, even into adulthood. Certainly, the effect on the quality of the relationship of a child with a parent would not be known completely until the latter reached the age of infirmity.

Research on day care for children also is confronted with almost insurmountable obstacles because of definitional, population selection, site, personnel, control group, duration, and compounding family variables. For example, even how day care is defined varies widely. A child might be in day care from one month to five years of age and for a duration of several to twelve hours a day.

Typical of studies demonstrating the benefits of day care is one of a model infant day-care center run by a school of education for children between the ages of two and twenty-two months for 20 hours a week. It reported the positive influence of day care on child-rearing at home (Edwards et al., 1987).

On the other hand, the adverse consequences of interrupting the attachment bonds by separating young children from their parents are well known to clinicians (Bowlby, 1980). The immediate effect is an insecure parent-child relationship. The widespread use of medications with insecure children and frustrated parents appear to be the result. A pertinent Swedish study of hospitalized children revealed that those who had received day care beginning at one year of age showed more anxiety-based behavior at the time of later hospitalization than did those who did not (Elander et al., 1986).

Teachers report that contemporary kindergartners look older and seem more mature, self-assured, and assertive than in the past; yet they are less self-disciplined. They show less interest in and respect for other children and teachers. Many exhibit symptoms of stress, low tolerance of frustration, and elevated aggressiveness (Zimiles, 1986, pp. 1-14). The heightened intensity of aggressive play reported by Carlsson-Paige & Leven (1988) could be a reflection of anger displaced from parents.

The evidence for a heightened incidence of contagious illnesses in children placed in institutional day care is mounting. For example, the hospitalization of infants and young children with serious lower-respiratory tract infections has been linked to day care outside of the home (Anderson et al., 1988).

Child psychiatrists see a vicious circle in which a child's separation anxiety is expressed by excessive seeking of parental attention when at home. This annoys the harried parent and produces growing strain between parent and child. The parent seeks more time away from the child, intensifying the child's provocative behavior. Parents, in turn, may experience feelings of guilt or loss for having placed their children in day care. In an effort to demonstrate their affection for their children, they may be overly permissive and work longer hours to purchase expensive toys and clothing as atonements.

The effect of interrupting attachment bonds during the first two years of life can be a failure to develop a basic trust in constant human relationships and an impaired ability to form committed relationships with other people (Magid and McKelvey, 1988). One long-term consequence is the alienation of teenagers from adults with resulting alcoholism, drug abuse, and suicide. More subtly, the legendary experience of the wealthy and royalty has been that children raised by surrogates are interested in their parents as sources of wealth and power rather than as persons. Early primary surrogate mothering entails the loss of that relationship for the child and possible alienation from, or idealization of, the child's biological mother (Hardin, 1985). Gloria Vanderbilt vividly described the adverse effects of such an occurrence in her life (Vanderbilt, 1985).

A review of the literature on infant day care in 1986 concluded that compensated infant-care leave was preferable to infant day care (Gamble & Zigler, 1986). That review suggested that even children who received quality infant day care are less socially responsive, less exploratory, and less attentive than those cared for by their parents.

The rapid expansion of day-care, preschool, and extended kindergarten programs has been accompanied by a widespread tendency to move the elementary school curriculum downward to younger children. In addition, many parents feel obligated to expose their children earlier to educational experiences. The result is what is now referred to as the "hot housing" movement for infants and toddlers devoted to expediting their development (Gallagher & Coche, 1987). This is occurring in spite of the evidence that the long-term outcomes of early didactic, authoritarian approaches with younger children relate negatively to intellectual achievement (Sigel, 1986 a & b).

The quality of child-parent relationships and the subtle emotional and personality effects of early life experience are exceedingly difficult to evaluate. Furthermore, the adverse effects of early life experience often are not evident for decades, and the problem of controlling all of the variables in child-rearing and the individual differences in children invalidates anything other than large-scale experiments that cannot be carried out in a democratic society.

Fortunately for us, other societies have tested the limits of adjusting the care of young children to traditional workplaces by institutionalizing infant day care so that parents could work on a full-time basis. The most notable were in nations with communal child-rearing objectives, such as Israel, the Soviet Union, Czechoslovakia, and the People's Republic of China. Even in these countries with strong ideological commitments to the full-time employment of parents and the group care of children, each attempt yielded to adjusting the workplace so that parents could care for their own babies during parenting leaves and return to their jobs with supplementary child care.

In order to gain an appreciation of the efforts expended historically and in other parts of the world to cope with equalization of gender roles and the full-time employment of parents, a summary of the experiences of the Israeli kibbutzim deserves attention:

> Dedicated to community living, the success of the first kibbutz, established in 1909, led to the growth of kibbutzim population levels to 117,999 (3.66 percent of the total Israeli Jewish population) in 1979 (Blasi, 1986). As with all other

aspects of kibbutz living, child care is undertaken as a community project. Just as social norms and concerns in the kibbutzim have changed with time, so have many of the principles guiding child care.

Early kibbutz mothers were strongly opposed to repeating their own experience as children, and they depreciated possessiveness and individualism. Consequently, children's houses were established, creating a separation of parents from children at birth. This initial extreme, which included breast feeding by mothers of other children, proved to defeat the kibbutz's goal of improved child-rearing because of parental unhappiness and stifling of the parent-child relationship. The current approach to child care in kibbutzim emphasizes frequent parent-child interaction in combination with communal care principles.

Contemporary kibbutz child care is separated into various levels according to the age of the child and associated developmental needs (Lewin, 1987). From birth to the age of eight weeks, the infant is cared for exclusively by the mother. The metapelet is a child-care professional who supports the infant's primary attachment to the mother. After eight weeks mothers begin to work four hours a day, gradually returning to work seven hours a day at the end of the first year. Babies stay overnight in their parents' apartment during the first year. About eighty percent of the kibbutzim children now sleep in their parents' apartments, and the children's houses are now day-care centers. The metapelet (ideally the same one who began working with the child) assumes a guiding role and is responsible for the training of the child in areas such as eating, dressing, and toilet training. Fathers help mothers care for their children during the afternoon and at night time. Between the ages of three and four years, children enter kindergarten.

The quality of child care is given high priority as is reflected in the kibbutz budget for children. Child-care nurses are trained in infant care as well as mother-infant relations. An educational committee, largely influenced by parents, chooses the metapelets for each children's house. The need for a cooperative working relationship between mother and permanent metapelet is clearly recognized.

Concern for parental welfare also is a component of the kibbutz child-care system. It is believed that the provision of child care allows parents to continue their productive role in life and avoids the tension and competition produced by child-care responsibilities. The goal is improved family life and more pleasurable encounters between the parents and children.

Concern over the impact of child-family separation prompted study in the 1960s. Rabin (1965) found a slight lag in intellectual and personality development in the first two to three years of life, which he attributed to frustration over the absence of the mother. His studies showed that kibbutz children at the age of ten showed greater emotional maturity, less sibling rivalry, less selfishness, and somewhat more anxiety and hostility toward their parents than non-kibbutz children. Subsequent awareness of the importance of child-parent relationships resulted in a shift toward supporting family relationships and families living together.

Infants and young children generally adjust to whatever is done to them, but there is growing suspicion that short- and long-term harm results from the institutional day care of infants and toddlers, if not in the form of actual emotional or personality damage, at least in the form of weak or ambivalent emotional ties to their parents. In either event, there may be resulting difficulty in finding and sustaining loving, committed relationships in later life and a lack of abiding attachments to their parents.

The Developmental Needs of Infants and Toddlers

Both children and adults need the basics in life—food, shelter, and love. In the United States, all but a glaring minority have food and shelter, but many are searching for love. The emphasis of the market place in our society is on being admired and implicitly being loved. Often absent is an awareness that the essential ingredient of being loved is the capacity to love others. More critical is the lack of awareness that in order to love as an adult one must have experienced being loved as a child. And, even more to the point is that the truly loved child is both the recipient of parental affection and parental limit-setting. For in order to love as an adult, a child needs to learn that respect for the source determines the value of love. Unreturned love demeans the importance of the one who loves. Accordingly, parents earn the love of their children by gaining their children's respect.

Children who are overindulged with parental attention often do not respect their parents nor return their parents' love.

Most parents intuitively recognize that the formation of attachment bonds with their babies during the early months of life is a time-consuming, intensely personal interaction. Since babies form attachments with whoever cares for them, the development of secure parent-child relationships depends upon babies' forming primary attachment bonds with their parents rather than temporary caregivers.

The attachment bonds of infants are their emotional lifelines and the foundation on which self-esteem builds. Since we cannot see these bonds, we infer their existence by observing certain behaviors considered to be "hallmarks of attachment." These are proximity-seeking and proximity-maintaining behaviors and protest responses under separation. Examples are the close following of a mother by a toddling child and the despairing cries of outrage when the mother goes away, and the child is prevented from accompanying her. Prior to toddlerhood, the baby enhances the mutual bonding process by smiling and by clinging to the person who embodies the essence of protection, security, and survival.

The attachment of baby animals to their mothers is guaranteed by interlocking instinctual messages and responses. The human instinctual patterns are less defined so that attachment is not guaranteed. This means that there are wide variations in patterns of parenting and modes of communication between human babies and their mothers (Fraiberg, 1987, p. 21). The bond is the product of a complex sequential development during the first 18 months of life. A dialogue occurs between infant and mother in which messages from the infant are interpreted by the mother, and messages from the mother are taken as signals by the baby.

It takes three to six months for infants and parents to establish regular feeding and sleeping patterns. During that time, infants are forming attachment bonds with familiar adults (Bowlby, 1969, 1973, and 1980). At about eight months of age, the baby demonstrates a clear recognition memory of the face of adults to whom the baby is bonding. In order for the recognition memory of bonding to take place, there must be an indelible tracing of the caregiver's face with its particular characteristics through countless repetitions associated with pleasure and need gratification (Fraiberg, 1987, p. 23). The attachment process between parent and infant really is falling in love. Two people arouse in each other sensual joy, feelings of longing, and the conviction that they are indispensable to each other (ibid., p. 32).

Because the loved parent is valued above all other things, a child gradually modifies aggressive impulses and finds alternative modes of expression that are sanctioned by love (ibid., pp. 12-15, p. 65). Children and adults who did not learn how to love during infancy contribute far beyond their numbers to social disorder. They are unable to fulfill the ordinary human obligations of work, friendship, marriage, and child-rearing. They contribute largely to the criminal population. The absence of human bonds leaves free "unbound" aggression to pursue its erratic course. Since these persons value no partner, anyone can be exchanged for any other without experiencing the pain of loss. In addition, some engage in brutal sexual and aggressive acts, as if the violent discharge of these drives becomes an affirmation of their importance.

Although birth mothers are favored by newborns because of their intrauterine relationships (Hoppers & Zigler, 1988), infants form bonds with any available and constant caregivers. While no one seriously denies that children need loving care and suffer from the lack or loss of it, a responsible case can be made for the view that a child's experience is enriched by regular interaction with a limited number of adults beyond the parents, each making their own contribution to the child's needs. For this reason, the parents of young children employed away from home should be the primary caregivers and make arrangements for their children to be cared for by others with whom they have good relationships (Goldthorpe, 1987, p. 55). Many children have more than one figure toward whom they direct attachment behavior; however, these figures are not treated alike. The primary caregiver holds a special place in the child's affections, distinct from the attachments to others. Michael Rutter (1981) suggested that up to four or five substitute caregiving figures can be tolerated in early childhood, if the primary attachment bond is with a parent. The point is that parents who delegate infant care should ensure the primacy of their relationships with their babies.

Employed parents often cannot guarantee this continuity of caregiving by a few stable individuals. Daily separations are an inevitable occurrence when the parent of a young child is employed away from home. The cognizance of the developmental needs of infants has resulted in a closer examination of the appropriateness of institutional day-care facilities. The attachment-bonding process between infant and mother that begins prior to birth provides for the development of the infant's secure relationship with the external world. Separation of a developing attachment relationship, such as by hospitalization, results in protest behavior as part of an anxiety reaction and may affect personality development (Molkind & Rutter, 1985, pp. 42-43). Even brief separations can affect young children who lack an appreciation of time and perceive any separation as permanent.

Most parents care about meeting their children's emotional needs; however, they have difficulty distinguishing significant separation anxiety from transient emotional upsets. Therefore, discerning the effect of day care on children is not easy. Because day-care centers generally reward group-oriented compliance, skill learning, and knowledge, a behaviorally mature "false" self may be reinforced, masking underlying loneliness and longing for one's parent. A child regarded as well-adjusted in a day-care center is one who does not demonstrate distressful behavior on parental separation and finds satisfaction in the material distractions available. The fact that crying on leaving and returning to a parent disappears often is interpreted as evidence that a child has adjusted well to day care. In fact, it may well be evidence that the child has adapted to stressful situations by entering a stage in which stress is masked or that the child has adapted by investing less in the parent. Unfortunately, the adverse effects of this kind of early life experience may not be evident in more overt ways for years.

Deliberations about the care of infants and young children should deal with the real issues that are less related to the developmental needs of the children and more related to how much stress children can tolerate and how little parents can do for them without harming them. These issues lie beneath the rationalizations that they are being given the best cognitive and emotional stimulation and the best in education to provide a competitive edge over other children. The fact is that parents are trying to meet their own financial and career needs and also raise their children as well as they can at the same time. Their concern is about the costs of trade-offs.

The most important question for parents really should not be how their child will compete in later educational and vocational activities, but rather what kind of relationship will that parent and that child have during the rest of their lives. The seeds for a close supportive, and mutually rewarding lifelong relationship are sewn during the early years of the parent-child relationship. The foundation for emotional bonding that establishes mutual trust is laid during the first year of life. The rancor, alienation, and strain of so many parent-child relationships evident in the past and today can be attributed to the lack of awareness on the part of both mothers and fathers that babies are interacting people who need more than feeding and diapering. Parents who treasured those early years have been rewarded by life-long, strong family bonds. Those who did not have been disappointed by offspring who have little need for them. The priority parents give to the beginning of life has a bearing on the priority children will give them later.

Child-rearing in the past by mothers who stayed at home and fathers who were breadwinners was not ideal in itself. The point is not simply that parents be homemakers; it is that parents be parents in the true sense of the word, and both enjoy and bear with the agony and ecstasy of growing up with their children. Simply staying at home is not enough. Children need the full range of spontaneous and intuitive interaction with adults who truly love them enough to sacrifice for them, to absorb their rage when frustrated, and to accept them for what they are. The fact that parenthood is a developmental phase with growth potential for adults often is overlooked. Many parents do not see themselves as growing with their children but simply as caregivers.

A constituency for representing the developmental needs of children could draw support from parents who want to grow with their children. Then the focus would not only be on a child's need to be with the parent, but also would be on a parent's need to be with the child. For their own social development, young children do not need full-time day care or nursery school, although three- or four-year-olds benefit from part-time group programs with a nursery rather than elementary-school orientation.

Day Care and Public Policies

Although day care has been available in this country since the 19th century, it always has been with the assumption that parents should arrange and pay for the care of their own children. At certain times of crisis, the Federal government has made limited exceptions. During the Great Depression, the Work Projects Administration sponsored day-care services for the children of its workers. During World War II, the Lanham Act provided funds for day-care centers and nursery schools for mothers who were called to work for the war effort. In the 1960's, Operation Head Start programs were begun for disadvantaged children. In 1971, however, the Child Development Act that would have provided more general child-care subsidies for welfare recipients and additional child-care facilities was vetoed by President Nixon.

Before legislators allocate funds that would endorse institutional care for infants and toddlers in this country, they should analyze exactly what they are trying to accomplish and examine the solutions that other countries have developed already. If we assume that the current trend of full-time employment for both mothers and fathers is going to continue, then the appropriate question is what choices can we offer parents so that they can meet the needs of their children while fulfilling their responsibilities to their employers. Because of the magnitude of the social and mental problems in the United States resulting from disrupted or disturbed parent-child relationships, all public policies that affect children must have as the first consideration strengthening, rather than undermining, parent-child relationships.

Self-interest and compromise, which generally determine the allocation of Federal funds, do not work well when children and human resources are at stake. None of the lobbyists are asking if institutional day-care programs will serve the developmental needs of children and parents, or if they will nurture and sustain the vital human connections of children, or if the compromises of special interest groups will compromise the interests of children.

Conservatives object to publicly funded day care on two general grounds. First, they believe that the best day-care provider is a mother at home. To relieve her of this traditional duty is demoralizing to her, to her children and to society, in this view. Second is the question of fairness. Tax-supported day care is seen as obliging mothers who prefer to care for their own children to pay for the care of children of often more prosperous women, who compete with their husbands in the labor market. The equity issue is illustrated by the following example (Samuelson, 1988):

> Child-care subsidies place government's authority behind
> one way of raising children. They imply that employed
> mothers deserve help, while those who stay at home do not.
> Consider two families who live next to each other. Each has
> two children, and the fathers work together and earn
> $20,000 apiece. In the first family, the mother works part-
> time and earns an additional $10,000. Her day-care
> expenses total $4,000, but the government pays $2,000.
> This is not a children's program. It is income redistribution
> that is unfair to the second family.

The only fair way to deal with this situation is to give the mother at home the same kind of child-care allowance received by the mother employed away from home, as is done in Canada and many European countries.

In European countries, the social response to infant care has been adjustment of the workplace to parenting rather than institutional day care because of declining labor forces in addition to the belief that society should share the costs of child-rearing. In contrast, in the United States parents have been forced to adjust to their workplaces because of an increasing labor pool that reduces the incentive of employers to accommodate to the needs of employees and the belief that parents alone should bear the costs of raising their children. Consequently, with the exception of some major corporations, neither private nor public sector workplaces in the United States have accommodated significantly to parenting. The incentive to do so may well increase in the future with a shrinking labor force and the realization that satisfied parents are reliable and productive employees.

In France, mothers are guaranteed four months of job-protected leaves, including up to six weeks before and ten weeks after birth. An additional job-protected unpaid leave is available to either parent for up to two years in companies with 100 or more employees. In Great Britain, mothers are entitled to an 18-week maternity leave with job protection. In Sweden, parents are entitled to one year of job protection with 90 percent of their salary for nine months and unpaid leave from 12 to 18 months.

In Czechoslovakia following World War II, the extensive group care of young children was arranged to permit virtual full employment of men and women (Langmeier & Matejcek, 1975). Because of the resulting social problems, this practice was reversed by the Family Code of 1964 that was further improved by a 1983 amendment containing a detailed set of provisions for protecting and supporting motherhood, the family, and children (Havlicek & Machacek, 1986). Currently, employed women receive ninety percent of their salary for twenty-six weeks. Subsequently, they are paid a maternity benefit until their child is two years old. Moreover, a lump-sum benefit is paid to a woman on the birth of every child.

In the United States a "macho" attitude contributes to the sentiment that parents and babies will cope with separations from each other. There are resilient children who seem to adjust to unusual life stresses, and there are women who can successfully cope with the conflicting demands of career and family (Blum, 1983). They are exceptionally hard working and exceptionally competent. There also are gifted adults who are able to nurture children in day-care centers without suffering from burnout, but there are children and women, perhaps the large majority, who are not so resilient. For them our society must create viable alternatives for careers and for child care.

A closer look at resilient children also is warranted. Their life stories reveal that competence, confidence, and caring can flourish, even under adverse circumstances, if young children encounter persons who provide them with a secure basis for the development of trust, autonomy, and initiative (Werner, 1989). They have had at least one person in their lives who consistently accepted them unconditionally, regardless of temperamental idiosyncracies, physical attractiveness, or intelligence. From this evidence it is better to strengthen such available ties to kin for high-risk children than to introduce additional layers of bureaucracy into the delivery of services for them in institutional day care. In those instances when day care is advocated because children are better off there than with their parents, the question is raised as to whether the best course from the child and parent's point of view is treatment of the parent-child unit, foster placement of the child, or termination of parental rights and adoption. The most effective interventions to prevent the maladjustment of young children stress the continuing, active involvement of parents. Parental participation not only benefits the child directly but also increases the parent's own self-concept, autonomy, and sense of competence (Rickel & Allen, 1987).

Finding the range of alternatives needed to meet the variety of family and employment requirements necessitates rethinking of society's priorities so that men and women are truly equals; solutions are based on the needs of children; and parents fully acknowledge their responsibilities to raise their children. Having a child involves a physical, moral, intellectual, emotional, and financial commitment to take care of that child. Taking care of a child often entails personal and professional trade-offs, even sacrifices. All of these trade-offs and sacrifices would be less severe if both parents made them as equal partners (Blum, 1983).

Being able to have everything we want is a prevalent theme of today's consumer-oriented society. Consequently, many young parents are frustrated when they encounter the unexpected complexities of pursuing occupational, career, financial, and child-rearing goals at the same time. The resulting stress further complicates their lives, and relief may be sought in drugs, alcohol, and diversionary activities that take priority over relationships with their children.

Raising children is work, whether it is done by a mother, by a father, by a relative, by a family day-care provider, by an at-home sitter, by a day-care center, or by a combination of them (Blum, 1983). It can be boring, frustrating, lonely, fatiguing, thankless, repetitive, and even claustrophobic. It also can be warm, stimulating, satisfying, challenging, and joyful. Inevitably, child-rearing is a fleeting experience through which children rapidly pass. Society must redefine and reevaluate child-rearing so that it is not demeaned as being without financial value. The high short-and long-term cost of replacing parents highlights the real economic value of parenting.

If men and women desire to have children, they must decide how they are going to raise them and how they are going to pay for it (Blum, 1983). When couples do reproduce, they should do so with what Erik Erikson calls generativity—concern about establishing and guiding the next generation (Erikson, 1963). He pointed out that wanting or having children does not automatically produce generativity. A child needs a healthy, secure, consistent, loving, disciplined, unpressured infancy and childhood. It is primarily the responsibility of parents to so provide. It is the responsibility of society to create structures and policies that enable parents to do so. These structures and policies must be attractive, viable, and equitable for both men and women (Blum, 1983).

If parents feel that they cannot afford to live on one salary, they should rethink their priorities (Blum, 1983). No one wants to reduce their economic status, but sometimes it is necessary. In an era of trade-offs, parents should be able to decide that they have to sacrifice for their family. When parents cannot afford or do not want to give up some career time to raise their children, they must be prepared to value and respect the persons whom they employ to do that work for them. When parents have positions in which much of the work can be done at home and there is enough flexibility for emergencies, then they have a relatively easy solution. However, if both careers are not adaptable, parents must explore options for the routine as well as the sick care of children. Under ideal circumstances, child care is an extension of the family in the community. That formerly was, and still is for many, a neighborly function. For parents who have a choice, therefore, living in environments suitable for children is important.

The overlooked essence of child care is that it is purchasing more than a place for physical care, scheduled activities, and supervision. It is purchasing adult guidance and friendships for one's child. That fact introduces a whole range of considerations about the kind of person who is giving the care and about whether love can be purchased. A natural love for babies and young children is the most important ingredient of quality child care. With a vested interest in the child at stake, parental love and attention is given without an automatic association of reward or payment for services rendered. It is not easy, if ever possible, to obtain that kind of devotion from other adults. Quality day care also means play, conversation, and comfort with persons of whom the child is fond and can know over extended periods of time (Galinsky, 1986; Rutter, 1981).

The professionalization of parenting is seen in the promotion of day care as preferable to home care. However, it is unrealistic to expect that psychology can ever offer ready-made technology for socialization. The child-rearing tasks remain an intuitive art of dealing with an enormously complex dialectic process in nature requiring not only knowledge but creativity. The commercial promotion of freestanding infant and toddler day care presents a double-pronged danger. It both attracts parents away from their babies and reduces the pressure to make the needed adjustments of the workplace to permit parents to care for their own children.

The assumption that both parents always will be employed full-time in traditional ways and settings is both shortsighted and false. It is popular today to say that the future holds more and more parents employed in traditional jobs, so that we must provide more places for children to be away from home and more professionally trained people to care for them. This view forecasts a new era of nonparental child rearing as an improvement over the past suburban two-parent home with male breadwinner and female housewife with two children.

The facts are to the contrary. First of all, the nuclear family image is a mythical product of post-World War II consumerism promoted by the builders of housing, manufacturers supplying single-family houses, automobile manufacturers, and a host of other industries that catered to freestanding living quarters. Second, the contemporary image of children living without two parents is contradicted by the fact that seventy-seven percent do live with two parents now (U.S. Bureau of the Census, 1988).

Most importantly, the workplace is in a state of continual flux. The post-agricultural emphasis yielded to industrial manufacturing which is now yielding to service industries. The advent of telecommunication promises even more dramatic changes in work styles offering greater opportunities for parents to combine employment and parenting. Technology is facilitating flexibility in work location, hours, and scheduling that will greatly benefit employed parents. Futurists, like Alvin Toffler, predict that by the 21st century, computer technology will reverse the urbanization spawned by the Industrial Revolution and create a society of home-based workers (Toffler, 1980). Even in 1987, the number of home-based professionals totaled 9,000,000 and is expected to rise to 13,000,000 by 1990, or over eleven percent of the U.S. work force. Because of their increased productivity, the fastest growing category is of telecommuters— homebound but salaried workers. For example, the Mountain Bell Telephone Company claims that its telecommuters are 35 percent to 40 percent more productive than other workers (*Time*, Oct. 26, 1987).

An important demographic factor that will influence the future labor market is the smaller number of adults following the "baby boom." For example, throughout the 1970's greater numbers of 23-year-olds surged into adulthood each year, peaking in 1983 at 4.4 million and since declining. This means that the future reduced labor force will provide an incentive for businesses to accommodate to the requirements of parents and their children.

Of equal significance is a shift away from a materialistic orientation to life. The importance of children is being recognized, so that more parents are giving higher priority to their families than to earned income. The older age of childbearing for many women and men has brought home the fact that there are seasons in life for their education, career development, child rearing, and financial gain.

For parents who choose to raise their children themselves, there should be rewards not penalties (Blum, 1983). If one parent chooses to take time off to raise a child, or if parents wish to share in that effort, they should have reassurances about resumption of employment without loss of seniority. There could be mechanisms within our employment and social-security systems so that those who do stay home to raise the children are considered employed and are accepted as contributing to the greater good of the entire community. Child-rearing allowances and tax benefits are tangible evidences of a society's commitment to children.

Many corporations have found that child-care benefits for their employees reduce absenteeism and increase productivity in addition to attracting more women to the work force. Employers can offer more flexibility in terms of hours, work weeks, extended training and promotion ladders, part-time employment, job sharing, and fringe benefits. There can be options for sick-child care, for extended maternity and paternity leaves, and for the care of children during school vacations. A 1984 survey of the Fortune 500 companies revealed that half of them had unpaid maternity leaves ranging from one week to six months (Finklestein, 1987). A 1987 survey of 10,345 U.S. companies by the U.S. Department of Labor revealed that 61 percent had specific policies, such as flexitime, to make child care easier, and 11 percent offered day care or other benefits related to child care (Saltzman & Barry, 1988).

In 1985, the Advisory Committee on Infant Care Leave recommended that infant-care leaves should be available for a minimum of six months, with partial income replacement included for three months and benefit continuation and job protection available for the entire six months leave period (Zigler & Frank, 1988). Parenting leaves are preferable to infant day care because they permit parents and infants to form attachment bonds with each other, to establish sleep and feeding patterns, and to recover from the stress of adding another person to the family (Hopper & Zigler, 1988). All of these options can be available to both fathers and mothers.

On-site employer-provided day care can be offered as a benefit to employees, and the cost of providing for such day care can be taken into consideration in determining an employee's salary (Blum, 1983). Since an employer-established day-care facility often can be run for less money than a freestanding facility, the use for the facility can be negotiated as a benefit rather than coming out of an employee's paycheck. From a tax standpoint, such an arrangement can save the employee money as well. Smaller employers can band together to form a day-care facility or contract with a nearby, freestanding center. Either arrangement allows stricter control over the quality of day care by the employer and employee without additional government regulation or involvement. Such an organized group of clients can have more influence on the management of the day-care facility than do individual parents.

There are two resources that should be considered in meeting the need for child care. One is the able elderly who are fully capable of being involved in volunteer work and are eager to do so. Many are experienced with children and would enrich the child-care system from their own lives and experiences. They would gain a real sense of worth and satisfaction from part-time assistance in day-care centers (Fallows, 1985, pp. 181-182).

The other resource is young people who could assist in the rough-and-tumble activities young children require. High-school students would gain a more realistic picture of parenting through such exposure in connection with family education. More substantially, the establishment of a national service obligation of one to two years for every man and woman over 18 years of age could have day-care work as one of the options. For day-care centers, it could offer entry-level staff committed to a term of service that exceeds the current temporary status of most beginning day-care workers.

Society's Stake in Child Care

The contemporary day-care movement raises issues that challenge basic cultural values. The magnitude of the controversy it has stirred up points to the emergence of social values that conflict with cultural values. In order to place the controversy in perspective, it is helpful to distinguish between social and cultural values. Employing the metaphor of a tree, society is represented by the leaves that carry on essential life processes that change with the seasons, and culture is represented by the trunk and roots that provide the underlying structure and nourishment.

Social values are the product of contemporary life styles and address the issues of day-to-day living within the organizational structures of society. They are strongly influenced by technology, because they are concerned with the survival of individual members of the species and enhance physical comforts. The societal objectives of child-rearing in the United States are to produce consumers, who also are competent and productive, and to produce educated citizens, who can make informed decisions intelligently.

In contrast to social values which are transient, cultural values endure over generations and ensure the survival of the species. Cultural values that support harmonious group living and social order are biologically based in family structures. Thus, they provide meaning and purpose for life in terms of species survival. The child-rearing objectives of the American culture are producing creative, autonomous, responsible persons capable of committed attachments to others and contributing to the common good.

Society and culture are interdependent. Our society needs adults who are committed to the goals of the commonwealth. This is furthered by our culture's emphasis upon committed attachment to others. Because social values are implemented through the policies of the government, they cannot provide the infrastructure of human relationships needed to ensure commitment to the common good. The human community depends upon cultural values mediated through cultural institutions of which the family is the centerpiece.

Without the support of cultural values, social values cannot endure. When a social and a cultural value conflict, the usual result is short-range dominance of the social value, ensuing controversy, and long-range prevailing of the cultural value.

In recent decades, social values in the United States have stressed materialism and individualism. The importance of committed human relationships and family life has been obscured. Business for profit and the working life have been adulated. The resulting conflict between social and cultural values has been devaluation of parental nurturing and of commitment to babies and toddlers, which may affect the quality and stability of the child's human attachments in ways that cannot yet be predicted fully. It is of interest to note, however, that the overriding emphasis on materialism in the United States has not been accompanied by the economic success and quality of life achieved in some other societies.

In many European countries, social and cultural values are less discordant; employment and family life are seen as equally essential and mutually complementary elements of society. Therefore, the prevailing attitude there is that the government and private industry must be sensitive and make concessions to the ever-present needs of employed parents and their children. In the United States, most employers expect parents to act exactly the same as childless employees and have strongly resisted child-care leaves. This expectation is a holdover from a time when few women worked, and most fathers had a wife who stayed home full time to care for the children. It is reinforced by childless workers who feel that child-related benefits discriminate against them. For them, profamily legislative proposals tend to be construed as "anti-everything else" (Kilpatrick, 1987).

Many aspects of society in the United States do not support family life (Kagan et al., 1987). There is an impoverishment of the sense of community and of personal intimacy, as materialism and competitiveness are over-emphasized. Parenthetically, the rewarding of materialistically oriented activities and achievements in many day-care programs today may propagate this dehumanizing emphasis. Only a strengthening of genuine closeness and connectedness in the family and community can reverse this trend. Changing traditional gender roles need not diminish the capacities for friendships, love, and family relationships.

The objectives of child-rearing are not susceptible to controlled experimentation and the manipulation of variables. Rather they flow from the overall aims of a society and culture. The equalization of male and female social roles was an important ideological goal for the Zionist movement in Israel and socialist revolutions in the Soviet Union and China. The efforts of each of these societies to replace parents with child caregivers failed, so that the ultimate result was accommodating workplaces to parenting with extended maternity and paternity leaves and job guarantees. These social experiments were corrected because of the commitment of those societies to child-rearing goals. The values of their respective cultures prevailed over transient social values.

In contrast, the United States has not clearly articulated its social and cultural goals for its children. The general assumption is that parents will raise their children as they wish, although there are expectations that children will be educated. However, the lack of articulated societal goals for child-rearing in the United States does not mean that they do not exist at a deeper level in our culture. As our society becomes more involved in child-rearing, these goals are being codified in legislation that affects children. The expectation that children will become competent, committed, and compassionate citizens seems clear, in that order of desirability. We expect adults to be competent in their work and citizenship responsibilities. We expect adults to be reliable and to honor their obligations to others. Especially within families, we expect people to care about each other.

In the United States, there is a fundamental emphasis on the autonomy of both adults and children in contrast with other social systems that weigh one more than the other. In this context the overall aim of child-rearing in the United States is the balanced development of an individual's potential to enable competent functioning within our social structure and economic system. The salient qualities needed to achieve this level of competent functioning are social skills, which include the ability to communicate, relate, and be useful to others and the capacity for assuming personal responsibility for self-expression, decision-making, and independent living. No society has been able to achieve these expectations without parent-child emotional attachments supported by cultural values. Among other things, the current dilemma over the institutional care of infants and toddlers is a manifestation of a conflict between our society's valuation of paid employment and our culture's commitment to parent-child attachments.

Conclusion

There are no easy answers to the problems of child care for parents employed away from home. Those who claim there are deceive both themselves and the public. They denigrate child development as well as child care. They minimize the role of the family in our culture. They overlook the historical expectation that in times of transition or stress women and children make the first trade-offs and the compromises (Blum, 1983).

On the positive side, day care permits parents to obtain fulfillment in their careers and increased income. Children are exposed to the broader community of adults and peers and enriched in knowledge and skill development. The visibility of groups of young children in communities serves as a tangible reminder that children are a part of society. Employment opportunities for adults, including youth and the elderly, are increased. In general the children are exposed to relatively consistent limit-setting and environments, and government is involved in monitoring the quality of care of young children.

On the negative side, parents are enticed away from the mutually rewarding formation of attachment bonds with their young children. Infants and toddlers are exposed to repeated separations from their parents and dilute their personal attachments. Children are programmed in groups managed by adults but dominated by peers. They lack intimate interactions with adults, the freedom to explore, and uninterrupted solitude. They are continually exposed to contagious illnesses. Most importantly, the weight of the evidence is that full-time day care of young children is contrary to their developmental interests.

In sum, the benefits of day care are clearly in the short-term interests of adults employed away from home and employers. The liabilities are in the long-term interests of children, parents, and society. The challenge for employers and public planners who are dominated by short-range rather than long-term considerations is to recognize that family life affects productivity and that the children of today are tomorrow's workers. Optimal development in childhood is related to future productivity in the labor market. Unfortunately, this leads to the conclusion in the minds of some that professional child-rearing is better than parenting. Consequently, someone must state the obvious: generally speaking, parenting is the best way of insuring optimal development in early life—children need parents.

In formulating national policies for the care of young children, it is essential that the primacy of the parent-child relationship be supported rather than undermined. For this reason, policies that enable parents to rear their own children are in the long-range interests of the children, their parents, and society. Conversely, policies that favor nonparental care of young children are contrary to these long-range interests. Rather than focusing solely on economic issues, national policies should focus on the quality of parent-child relationships. Short-term research on the benefits of day care for young children is not a reliable basis for policy formulation.

At the present time, national policies in the United States do not clearly support the family rearing of children. Even though we have one of the highest rates of mothers with children under the age of three in the labor force, the United States stands alone among industrialized nations in having inadequate statutory parental leave policies (Zigler & Muenchow, 1983). Unlike other countries, including Canada, Great Britain, France, and West Germany, the United States does not guarantee parents the right to leave work for enough time to care for their babies and income benefits to help compensate them if they do so. Parental leave policies not only support parental child-rearing, but they also reduce the cost of public assistance to unemployed parents, reduce the loss of productivity, and reduce the cost of retraining to employers (Spalter-Roth & Hartmann, 1988).

The challenge for parents is to find an optimal balance between the priorities of their families and their jobs. Both cannot be the first at the same time. The priority we give to our children in early life influences the priority they will give to us in later life. A shift in social values is needed to help fathers recognize their importance in child-rearing. Men are learning that nurturing relationships with children can be fulfilling for them (Pruett, 1987, p. 280). In order to further this awareness, boys need opportunities to help care for babies and young children (Brazelton, 1985, p. xxii). The ultimate reward for both mothers and fathers is that children grow into balanced, flourishing individuals who identify with both sides of their parents—the working and the nurturing (ibid., p. 190). Too many parents find that when they finally have time to spend with them, the children have grown up and have no time for them.

In the past, only one breadwinner in a family was needed. Now many parents feel that two incomes are needed to support their families. This reflects both a real diminution in the purchasing power of the dollar and higher material expectations. Many could manage on less income, if they were fully aware of the importance of the early years of their children's lives to both them and their children. The widespread search for meaning and fulfillment in life is a symptom of the failure of many adults to find satisfaction in their family lives, which often have been dominated by busy activities or spoiled by strained and disrupted relationships.

The challenge for society is to recognize the social value of parenthood and to support rather than undermine family life. Because children are vital to the survival of society, someone will have to nurture and protect them. Both parents and the larger society will have to pay for that care.

Full-time day care, no matter how heavily funded, is not in the interests of young children, their parents, or society, because it is a response to the employment of parents in traditional workplaces by necessity or choice, not to the needs of the children nor of the parents. Attention to meeting the developmental needs of children and of parents who want to be with them opens the door to various ways of adapting workplaces to parents and children. The central question is whether the care of infants and toddlers should conform to traditional workplaces or whether workplaces should adapt to permit parents to care for their own children. The future of our society depends on the welfare of young children during the years in which they are learning to trust, respect, and depend upon adults—the foundation for later citizenship and productivity. We should help parents find ways through workplace adjustments, family benefits, and tax adjustments to parent their own young children.

Our evolving society must place a high priority on child-rearing or face losing its leadership in world affairs. There are few limits to what can be done *to* children. The question is what needs to be done *for* them to ensure the kind of life we seek for them.

—Jack C. Westman is professor of psychiatry at the University of Wisconsin—Madison.

Grateful acknowledgment is made to Marcia Slattery for her assistance in assembling material and to Stephen Small for his editorial comments.

REFERENCES

Anderson, Larry J.; Parker, Robert A.; Stikas, Raymond A.; Farrar, Jeffrey A.; Gangarosa, Eugene J.; Keyserling, Harry L.; & Sikes, R. Keith (1988) "Day-Care Center Attendance and Hospitalization for Lower Respiratory Tract Infections." *Pediatrics*. 82:300-308.

Blasi, Joseph (1986) *The Communal Experience of the Kibbutz*. New Brunswick, New Jersey: Transaction Books.

Blum, Marian (1983) *The Day Care Dilemma*. Lexington, Massachusetts: Lexington Books.

Bowlby, John (1969, 1973, & 1980) *Attachment and Loss,* Volumes I, II and III. New York: Basic Books.

Brazelton, T. Berry (1985) *Working and Caring*. Reading, MA: Addison-Wesley Publishing Co.

Briggs, Jr., V.M. (1987) "The Growth and Composition of the U.S. Labor Force." *Science* 238: 176-180.

Carlsson-Paige, Nancy & Leven, Diane E. (1988) *The War Play Dilemma*. New York: Teachers College Press.

Conniff, Dorothy (1988) "Is Junior in Good Hands?" *Isthmus* November 4.

Cummings, E. Mark & Beagles-Ross, Jessica (1984) "Toward a Model of Infant Day Care: Studies of Factors Influencing Responding to Separation in Day Care." In Ainslie, Ricardo C. (Ed.) *The Child and the Day Care Setting: Qualitative Variations and Development*. New York: Praeger.

Davidson, Christine (1988) *Staying Home Instead*. Levington, MA: Lexington Books.

Davis, Minnie (1988) *Ideal Motherhood*. Boston: Crewell, p. 29.

Dreskin, William and Wendy (1983) *The Day Care Decision*. Evans & Co.

Edwards, C.P., Logue, M.E., Loehr, S.R., & Roth, S.B. (1987) "The Effects of Day Care Participation on Parent-Infant Interaction at Home." *American Journal of Orthopsychiatry* 57: 116-119.

Elander, G., Nilsson, A., & Lindberg, T. (1986) "Behavior in Four-Year-Olds Who Have Experienced Hospitalization and Day Care." *American Journal of Orthopsychiatry* 56:612-616.

Erikson, Erik (1963) *Childhood and Society, 2nd Edition*. New York: Norton.

Fallows, Deborah (1985) *A Mother's Work*. Boston, MA: Houghton-Mifflin.

Finkelstein, A. (1987) "Parental Leave: A Policy for the Future." *Parents*. September: 240-242.

Fraiber, J.S. (1977) *Every Child's Birthright*. New York: Basic Books.

Gallagher, J.M. & Coche, J. (1987) "Hothousing: The Clinical and Educational Concerns Over Pressuring Young Children." *Early Childhood Research Quarterly*. 2:203-210.

Gamble, T.J. & Ziegler, E. (1986) "Effects of Infant Day Care: Another Look at the Evidence." *American Journal of Orthopsychiatry*. 56:26-42.

Gordon, L. (1988) *Heroes of Their Own Lives*. New York: Viking.

Graubard, Stephen R. (1987) "Preface to Learning About Women: Gender, Politics, and Power." *Daedalus*. 116:v-xx.

Gunzenhauser, N. & Caldwell, B.M., *Group Care for Young Children*. Skillman, NJ: Johnson & Johnson Baby Products, 1986.

Hardin, H.T. (1985) "On the Vicissitudes of Early Primary Surrogate Mothering." *Journal of the American Psychoanalytic Association*. 33:609-629.

Havlicek, K. & Machacek, D. (1986) *Life of the Youth in Czechoslovakia*. Prague: Orbis Press Agency.

Hopper, P. & Zigler, E. (1988) "The Medical and Social Science Basis for a National Infant Care Leave Policy." *American Journal of Orthopsychiatry*. 58:324-338. Hume, Katie (1988) "Children." *Time*, August 8, 1988, p. 36.

Kagan, Sharon L., Powell, Douglas R., Weissbourd, Bernice, Zigler, Edward F. (Eds.) (1987) *America's Family Support Programs: Perspectives and Prospects*. New Haven, CT: Yale University Press.

Kamerman, S.B. (1980) *Parenting in an Unresponsive Society.* New York: Free Press.

Kilpatrick, J.J. (1987) "Togetherness Law a Bad Seed." *Wisconsin State Journal.* November 9, 1987.

Kuhn, T.S. (1977) *The Essential Tension: Selected Studies in Scientific Tradition and Change.* Chicago, IL: University of Chicago Press.

Langmeir, J. & Matejcek, Z. (1975) *Psychological Deprivation in Childhood.* New York: John Wiley & Sons.

Levy, Frank (1987) *Dollars and Dreams.* New York: Russell Sage.

Lewin, G. (1987) Personal Communication. The School of Education of the Kibbutz Movement. Tivon, Israel.

Magid, Ken & McKelvey, Carole A. (1988) *High Risk: Children Without a Conscience.* New York: Bantam Books.

Mead, Margaret (1954) "Some Theoretical Considerations on the Problem of Mother-Child Separation." *American Journal of Orthopsychiatry,* 24:477.

Mead, Margaret (1962) "A Cultural Anthropologist's Approach to Maternal Deprivation." In Ainsworth, M. (Ed.) *Deprivation of Maternal Care.* Geneva: WHO.

Morgan, Gwen (1987) *The National State of Child Care Regulation—1986.* Watertown, MA: Work/Family Directions, Inc.

Orwell, George (1961) *1984—A Novel.* New York: New American Library.

Physician Survey (1985) "The Two Career Family." *Medical Aspects of Human Sexuality.* 19:43-51.

Pogrebin, L.C. (1983) *Family Politics.* New York: McGraw-Hill.

Pruett, Kyle D. (1987) *The Nurturing Father.* New York: Warner Books.

Rickel, H. & Allen, L. (1987) *Preventing Maladjustment from Infancy Through Adolescence.* Newberry Park, CA: Sage Publications.

Rositer, B.A. (1982) *A Developmental Guide to Starting an Infant or Toddler in Day Care: Obtaining the Benefits While Dealing with the Problems.* Pittsburgh, PA: Louise Child Care Center.

Rutter, Michael (1981) "Social-emotional Consequences of Day Care for Preschool Children." *American Journal of Orthopsychiatry,* 51: 4-28.

Rutter, Michael (1982) "Prevention of Children's Psychosocial Disorders: Myth and Substance." *Pediatrics* 70:883-894.

Saltzman, Amy & Barry, Patrick (1988) "Child Care and Fathers." *U.S. News and World Report.* June 20, 1988.

Samuelson, Robert J. (1988) "The Debate Over Day Care." *Newsweek,* June 27, 1988.

Sigel, I.E. (1986a) "Early Social Experience and the Development of Representational Competence." In Fowler, W. (Ed.) *Early Experience and the Development of Competence.* San Francisco: Jossey-Bass, pp. 49-65.

Sigel, I.E. (1986b) "Reflections on the Belief-Behavior Connection: Lessons Learned from a Research Program on Parental Belief Systems and Teaching Strategies." In Ashmore, R.D. & Brodzinsky, D.M. (Eds.) *Thinking About the Family: Views of Parents and Children.* Hillsdale, NJ: Erlbaum, pp. 35-65.

Slater, Philip (1970) *The Pursuit of Loneliness.* Boston: Beacon Press.

Spalter-Roth, Roberta M. & Hartmann, Heidi I. (1988) *Unnecessary Losses.* Washington, D.C.: Women's Policy Research Institute.

Toffler, A. (1980) *The Third Wave.* New York: William Morrow & Co.

U.S. Bureau of the Census (1987) *Who's Minding the Kids?* Washington, D.C.: U.S. Government Printing Office.

U.S. Bureau of the Census (1988) *Household Families, Marital Status, and Living Arrangements,* p. 20 No. 432. Washington, D.C.: U.S. Government Printing Office.

Vanderbilt, G. (1985) *Once Upon a time*. New York: Alfred A. Knopf.

Ward, Angela (1988) "A Feminist Mystique." *Newsweek*, September 12.

Webb, Nancy Boyd (1984) *Preschool Children with Working Parents*. New York: University Press of America, 1984.

Werner, Emmy E. (1989) "Protective Factors and Individual Resilience." In Mosels, S.J. & Schonkoff, M. (Eds.) *Handbook of Early Intervention*.

Westman, Jack C. (1979) *Child Advocacy*. New York: Free Press.

Whiting, Beatrice (Ed.) (1963) *Six Cultures—Studies of Child Rearing*. New York: John Wiley.

Wolkind, Stephen, & Rutter, Michael (1985) "Separation, Loss and Family Relationships." In Rutter, Michael & Hersov, Lionel (Eds.) *Child and Adolescent Psychiatry*. Oxford, England: Blackwell.

Young, K.T., and Zigler, E. (1986) "Infant and Toddler Day Care: Regulation and Policy Interpretations." *American Journal of Orthopsychiatry* 56: 43-55.

Zigler, E. & Muenchow, S. (1983) "Infant Day Care and Infant Care Leaves: A Policy Vacuum." *American Psychologist*. 38: 91-94.

Zigler, E. & Frank, M. (1988) *The Parental Leave Crisis: Toward a National Policy*. New Haven, CT: Yale University Press.

Zimiles, H. (1986) "The Social Context of Early Childhood Education in an Era of Expanding Preschool Education." In Spodek, B. (Ed.) *Today's Kindergarten*. New York: Teachers College Press.

Participants in "Risks of Day Care" Consultation

December 6, 1988

Author of Paper

Jack Westman
Department of Psychiatry
University of Wisconsin Medical School
Madison, Wisconsin

Other Participants

Peter Barglow
Michael Reese Hospital
Chicago, Illinois

Jay Belsky
Department of Child Psychology
Pennsylvania State University
University Park, Pennsylvania

Marian Blum
Child Study Center
Wellesley College
Wellesley, Massachusetts

Allan Carlson
President
The Rockford Institute

Bryce Christensen
Director
The Rockford Institute Center on The Family in America

Brian Vaughn
Department of Psychology
University of Illinois
Chicago, Illinois

Burton White
Center for Parent Education
Newton, Massachusetts

Risks of Day Care: Summary of a Discussion

Day care was the subject for discussion among the eight researchers gathered at the Sheraton International at O'Hare outside Chicago, Illinois in December, 1988. Participants came from a number of different institutions and spoke from diverging political perspectives, yet all present had been engaged either in doing research on the effects of day care or in interpreting the social implications of such research. All present were likewise united in perceiving that day care poses risks for children, although participants disagreed both about the extent and character of those risks, about why those risks exist and, as a result, about the appropriate social response to such risks. The consultation began with an examination of a paper on day care by Professor Jack Westman (a revised version is published in this volume), but quickly opened onto topics not directly addressed by the paper.

Acting as chairman for the consultation, Allan Carlson tried to sketch out the historical context for the current day care debates. He noted that in 1935 the Committee on Economic Security (progenitor of the Social Security system) had stressed "the special benefits of maternal care" as the justification for a new government program aiding fatherless households. In contrast, when Congress enacted a welfare reform bill in 1988, "maternal care was no longer its central goal; indeed, in some ways it has become the problem. Welfare mothers are now to be put in work or in training while their small children are put in day care or some other program, often said to be superior to care provided by the poor mother at home."

Carlson also cited the increased use of day care by middle-class mothers, as married women have moved into the work force in recent decades. Because of such trends, political pressure has grown for a national system of day care. Yet Carlson counted himself among those who "question the headlong rush into social parenting, deny its historical inevitability and hold that the debate is not over yet. Public policy choices should be made from a full hearing of the facts, not forced by a stampede brought on by emotion, by panic, or by ideology." In particular, he felt that to date the risks of day care had received too little attention and hoped that those gathered could shed light on those risks.

Jack Westman began his summary of his paper on day care by alluding to a Gauguin painting, *Riders on the Beach*, depicting human figures riding horses in different directions. For him, this picture represented the emotional state of many contemporary adolescents who are detaching themselves from social commitments. The frequent failure of emotional bonds is creating widespread anxiety and pain about the future of children. Although parents' affectionate bonds to their children are rooted in procreative instincts essential to the survival of the species, those bonds are strained by new pressures from the economic situation, and a "mélange of factors connected with gender differences, feminism, and reactive responses from men."

Despite the strident rhetoric that makes it difficult to see what really is going on, Westman disputed the assertion that America has no culture and, therefore, no standards against which to measure child care. Although temporarily "overwhelmed by societal pressures, there are generally accepted cultural values that can be identified." For example, a cultural consensus on proper parental behavior allows states to frame statutes on parental abuse and courts to adjudicate custody disputes between divorced parents. Contemporary social objectives in child-rearing include that of producing competent people who can become productive consumers and who are committed to the work force. The deeper cultural challenge, however, is to foster the development of compassionate citizens with a commitment to the common good.

Westman identified ties across the generations—between grandparents and grandchildren—as socially desirable and lamented that "many people . . . live in circumstances of alienation from their own family members and are deprived in later life of these family ties that are so important to individuals." At a time when much of the research on day care is focused on short-range effects, the importance of long-term intergenerational bonds must not be forgotten. Social scientists, he continued, must remember their "onerous responsibility" to avoid misleading a public that will "latch on to any kind of study in order to support ideologically, emotionally, or commercially appealing conclusions." All day-care research should be framed within theoretical models, such as Kuhnian paradigms, that link observations to the objectives of child-rearing within a larger context.

As the appointed discussant for Westman's paper, Burton White began his response by noting general agreement with the paper, particularly praising the author for acknowledging "the epistemological complexities" of the issues. Reflecting on his own career shift 30 years ago from mechanical engineering to human development, White recalled that he was "absolutely stunned at the difference in epistemological standards." While applauding the broad inclusiveness of the paper, White expressed surprise that the prevalence of infectious diseases in day care had not been mentioned in the earlier version of the paper. Most researchers now agree that day care dramatically elevates the risk of infectious disease—especially respiratory illness and middle-ear infections. And although these simple problems are not life-threatening, they can pose "a serious threat to the development of children" by repeatedly impairing hearing and so retarding the language acquisition essential for educational progress and social acceptance.

White identified the first couple of years of life as "the core of the issue" in the debate over nonmaternal care. Older children do not require the same kind of attention. What must be remembered is that "the substitute care movement was created not because we were looking for a better way to raise children, but because parents had new needs," traceable to shifts in the culture and economy. Surveying the child-care industry, White pronounced it "a total disaster area," with "no feasible way of turning it into a model industry." Consequently, most families will find only "pretty poor substitutes" for parental care outside the home.

White complained of the difficulty of conducting an intelligent discussion of the day-care question. Media reporters accept the most dubious pronouncements on "quality" day care, while most state and Federal legislators haven't "the faintest hope" of understanding the issues. Clear thinking is further inhibited by the "extremely strong emotions, most especially guilt," evoked by the question of child care. "When you are overwhelmed by guilt, you don't tend to think very clearly or debate fairly."

Explaining his own "continuing resistance to people other than family raising children as a routine policy," White pointed to "the gap" between the best way to raise a child and the kinds of conditions found in virtually any substitute-care program. "The gap is so large in my perspective, that I continue to feel totally uncomfortable with it and totally willing to talk to this issue in public . . . even though it has cost me dearly from time to time." White concluded with an appeal for more efforts to reshape public thinking about child-rearing through television, radio, and print. Only the lack of sound public information can account for the large number of professional couples who now put one-month-old infants in substitute care, five days a week. The time is past for child-care specialists to be talking to other academics. Their task is now to educate the general public.

Jay Belsky began the open discussion by expressing mixed feelings about Professor Westman's paper. On the one hand he was impressed by the attempt to go beyond empirical data to "put pieces together and make some broad statements or implications about American society." But on the other hand, Belsky remained unconvinced as to the certainty of these judgements. Not written with the kind of analysis usually expected by research scientists, the paper offered the strengths—and suffered the weaknesses—of a paper by an historian, philosopher, literary critic, or cultural anthropologist. Intrigued by the notion that our child-rearing reflects our cultural goals, Belsky wondered just what those goals are. "What are we preparing our children for?" he asked. Allowing himself a moment of tentative conjecture, he saw "hints in the data" on insecurity, aggression, and noncompliance among the young that suggest that the "tides of culture" are running against lasting commitments and enduring alliances, leaving "everyone out for himself" more than ever before. Perhaps, he further speculated, "strong bonds [and] authentic selves are really idealized visions of the past; it's not what the future holds." In looking at day care as it currently exists in the United States and the patterns of behavior associated with extensive nonparental child care initiated in infancy, he raised the theoretic possibility that, despite our resistance, "the forces of time may be more wise than we are" and "history is preparing us for its future," while "only the naive" are preparing their children for lives of emotional security. This line of thought, Belsky stressed, was "completely speculation," not the fruit of research and investigation.

Brian Vaughn shared Belsky's reservations about the lack of empirical data in Westman's paper but felt even more strongly that this lack was a deficiency. "I may share some of the opinions that were expressed in Dr. Westman's paper, however, I am really uncomfortable using a document like that to endorse or even express those opinions in the face of an overwhelming vacuum of information." This lack of empirical substance made the paper almost impossible to critique.

Vaughn and Belsky both disputed Westman's assertion that the social sciences were still stuck with an essentially Newtonian research model. In his defense, Westman acknowledged the use of the "multi-variable approach," but was still struck by the lack of a "multi-system Kuhnian sort of paradigm" in social science research. Vaughn disagreed, asserting that there are "lots of paradigms available," citing particularly John Bowlby's paradigm of social development. White then entered the fray, stressing that many complexities of human life still escape explanation within the available models of human development.

Bryce Christensen tried to clarify matters by arguing that although many paradigms exist in the social sciences, it is often impossible to design empirical experiments to resolve differences between them. In many cases, these differences reflect non-rational commitments. Such commitments, he observed, often survive the discovery of "adverse data" in a way that the Newtonian outlook could not survive the famous eclipse observations that validated Einstein's theory. Christensen pointed to the debate over day care as illustration of the imperviousness of social commitments to empirical data.

Belsky countered that such imperviousness was evident on both sides of the debate. In particular, he detected a strong bias in *The Family in America* toward research uncovering "perils of day care." "I think it is easy to say that emotions are hot and everybody is biased . . . so I can be too." Belsky admitted the impossibility of researchers' fully avoiding their own social biases, but he urged all present to "work real hard" at rising above those biases.

Vaughn held out the possibility of doing disinterested research. "It doesn't make a bit of difference whether the empirical findings fall one way or the other; there is a large audience. . . . You can be perfectly without bias and still do this work."

Belsky agreed with Vaughn on this point, but Christensen invoked the judgment of Swedish social scientist Gunnar Myrdal that objectivity in the social sciences is impossible. What is possible is honesty about commitments, and candor about perspective. Belsky was not buying. "To be honest about your biases and then go along with them is to be no longer scientific." Belsky found it remarkable that people accuse him of changing his mind on day care. "The data changed, the data looked different, and I see lots of people ignoring the data and explaining it away. . . . If the goal of disciplining oneself isn't there, then its journalism, not science."

Carlson returned the discussion to the work of Bowlby, asking whether Bowlby had created an "objective paradigm." Belsky replied that objectivity is not a quality inhering in a theory, but is instead a characteristic of a researcher grappling with data. While Bowlby had provided "a robust theory," social scientists don't have "many major paradigms . . . since the fall of psychoanalysis." Instead, there is a wide array of "mini-theories of this and mini-theories of that." Belsky took hope from the quantity of "first-class research going on," predicting that "enough data will be generated . . . that sooner or later someone will come along with a framework to integrate it. . . . That's how Kuhn says scientific revolutions occur."

When queried by Westman as to the possibility of using social science to determine cultural goals, Belsky responded that some cultural anthropologists already are pursuing such work.

The mention of cultural goals renewed Carlson's curiosity in Belsky's speculation that parents are turning to day care because "they are indeed reading the signs, and the signs say community in any real sense is dead." In this interpretation, day care as provided in the U.S. today provides "a good training ground" for the challenge of an individualistic modern society in which the "old bonds of family, neighborhood, and community are increasingly irrelevant."

Although Belsky was "led to wonder if that is what may be going on at some level," Vaughn wouldn't accept this interpretation. In the course of interviewing participants in the Barglow, Vaughn and Molitor study (1987), he found none who offered this kind of rationale. But Belsky questioned whether parents needed to be explicitly aware of all the factors which may influence their utilization of nonparental child care arrangements. To illustrate the limits of parental self-awareness, he cited some predictions he had made on the basis of sociobiology about who does and who does not use day care. In accordance with sociobiological theory, it turns out that parents are least likely to place a child in day care if the child is male or if the child has few brothers and sisters and few cousins. Lending further support to the sociobiological thesis, the data showed that, compared to other children, "kids who are first grandchildren in the father's lineage were significantly less likely to be in day care for 20 hours a week." To further illustrate the power of sociobiology to lead to an "uncanny prediction," he noted that in his set of data he found four children who were not only first grandchildren but were first grandsons and *none of them* were in day care for more than twenty hours a week. Sociobiologists can explain this pattern as a protection of progeny, but Belsky doubted whether parents were consciously aware that they were protecting a first grandchild from risk.

Viewing the matter from a different perspective, Belsky again speculated that day care may now be part of "some cultural programming" which teaches children how to be "relational opportunists" in a world which increasingly requires such opportunism. By increasing their emotional insecurity and by fostering noncompliance and aggression, the day-care experience in contemporary America may prepare children to cope with their cultural future. Belsky cited experiments with monkeys that showed that the quality of maternal care depends heavily on the availability of resources and the need to forage for food. As resources become more scarce and unpredictable, parental nurturance and solicitude decrease.

When White called for a halt to this speculation, Belsky conceded that he needed much more research to prove or disprove his hypotheses about day care. Belsky was "spooked" by the preliminary accuracy of the sociobiological predictions, but he found his ideas of cultural development "too intriguing" to discard. Citing "interesting new findings" from his own lab work, Belsky noted that day care can foster the development of avoidance response among infants, considered to reflect disguised anger toward their parents. Such avoidance can be interpreted as evidence of "a false self," suggesting that such children may "become dissociated from their feelings, especially their negative feelings." Such dissociation may preclude the self-disclosure essential to intimacy. "Why would anybody do that to a child?" Belsky asked. "Maybe they know something about the world they are preparing their kids for—a world, for example, that has little tolerance for the expression of vulnerability and one in which expressed weakness will be taken advantage of."

White again warned of the risks of "grossly ill-founded" speculations about unconscious parental motives and futuristic views. In his view, there is "not a stitch" of evidence to support Belsky's broad conjectures. A short dispute ensued between Vaughn and White, then White and Belsky, as to the limits, costs, and interpretation of interviews with parents.

The debate over research methods brought Peter Barglow into the discussion with a comment on how differences in professional discipline affect our views. In particular, he identified a divergence between his own perspective as a gatherer of data and Westman's perspective as a clinician. He recalled one occasion when co-authors of a research article on day care persuaded him to go beyond the empirical data by including a sentence stating that "the child that is exposed to repeated separations interprets these repeated separations from the mother as a kind of rejection." Barglow confessed that he was "extremely uncomfortable" about that statement, since he really didn't have any idea how one-year-olds interpret repeated absences. "We were crucified for that statement," he ruefully recalled. In suggesting a research agenda for the future, Barglow suggested two different approaches: 1) gathering more empirical data and asking more questions 2) developing pragmatic strategies for achieving desired results ("Nuhr was fruchtbar ist wahr"—Only that which is fruitful is true).

Shifting from theories governing research to research itself, Belsky reported on two new day-care studies, a "good news" study that has been accepted for publication and another study that is "still struggling" to find publication because it is bad news. In the "bad news" study, researcher Deborah Vandell looked at a large number of middle-class 8-year-olds in Texas, finding a number of problems showing up among those with "extensive child care histories beginning the first year of life." In school achievement, in social behavior, in self-esteem, the children who had been in extensive nonmaternal care since their first year of life were worse off than peers who had received maternal care. In marked contrast the "good news" study out of Sweden—also looking at 8-year-olds—found none of these negative effects. Indeed, the Swedish study even seemed to find some developmental advantages for children who had received nonparental infant care. But Belsky stressed two critical differences between the Swedish and the Texan circumstances: first, none of the Swedish mothers returned to work before their children were six months old because Sweden guarantees paid maternity leave; second, while American day care is mediocre at best, Swedish day care is well-staffed and well-funded. Still, Belsky found it instructive that despite the availability of a system of high quality day care, Sweden has now extended its maternal leave from six months to one year, more because of family preference and economics than because of developmental psychology (i.e., the effects of child care on child development).

Westman voiced his skepticism about studies which look at the effects of day care upon children who are one, three, eight, or fourteen years old. The effects of day care on the "affectionate bonds" between parent and child may not be visible until the children are "old enough to be parents themselves and when their own parents reach a stage of infirmity." Westman also regretted the absence of any mention of other cultures and societies with day care experience.

Belsky welcomed the opportunity to consider other cultures. He complained that critics had argued that in technologically primitive societies, children receive non-maternal care from many people.

Such cultural patterns are cited as evidence that it does not have to be mothers staying home full time. Belsky countered that such arguments are "right but wrong." Usually, in such cultures the baby sleeps with the mother all night long, nursing on demand, even if someone other than the mother provides daytime care. Second, whoever is providing for the baby is part of a permanent social structure, allowing the development of an enduring relationship. Invariably, a biological relation—an aunt, uncle, or sibling—is close to the baby. Such primitive societies do not "just let anybody" take care of the baby and "then just change these people off so there are no enduring bonds."

A dispute ensued about the possibility of identifying the emotional effects of day care 50 or 60 years later, with White and Barglow expressing deep skepticism, while Vaughn and Belsky were more hopeful, though mindful of the difficulties.

Although "not a research scientist," Marian Blum felt compelled to share her work in the trenches with children, with parents and teachers. That work had convinced her that infants and preschoolers are not the only ones at risk. "If you go to an after-school program at 4:30 in the afternoon when eight-year-old kids have been there since 7:30 in the morning, you see things that might not show up in a laboratory situation but which give me a great deal of concern about how we are treating our kids and what we are raising them for."

Belsky suggested that in recent work on programs designed for "latch key" children, researchers were finding that parental motivations for using such programs might be the most important influence in determining their outcomes for children.

Again emphasizing the limits of social science, Christensen asserted that family choices may often be traced to a religious metaphor beyond the reach of formulae. Recalling Richard Weaver's argument that those who do not care about their ancestors will not care about their posterity, Christensen recounted his own discovery of the remarkable linkage between the drop in Catholic fertility and the declining requests for memorial masses for the dead. "You probably couldn't get that into a social science journal . . . but somehow it says to me that the metaphor that Catholics are living by is different and it shows up at the two end points of life."

Belsky was not so sure that such patterns could not be studied through social science. Christensen agreed in part, but countered that science could not teach parents how to make sacrifices for their children but that contemplating certain religious metaphors could foster sacrifice. Stressing the difference between a scientific education which "equips the ego" and a moral education which "shapes the ego," he drew attention to the semantic tension in Westman's earlier calls both for "sacrifice" and for "competent consumers." "I think that the language of 'sacrifice' jostles very nervously against the language of 'competent consumers,'" he concluded.

Belsky protested that it was a mistake to suppose that "science is or should be expected to direct one's life. It's part of the data in the complex equation of culture." Christensen and Westman both strongly agreed.

Exploring further the relationship between science and society, Belsky complained of some colleagues who tell him that he ought not to say what he does about day care because other people might use his pronouncements to their own ends. Social scientists need to resist this kind of censorship vigorously as a violation of "everything we think of as basic to American life." Researchers should simply publish their findings, regardless of what "spin" others might put on those findings.

Westman urged that scientists recognize "an ethical obligation" to educate the public on the limits of their work. "Right now," he warned, "social science research reported by the media is being interpreted as gospel."

Vaughn questioned this assessment, pointing to the wide diversity of opinion on day care among research scientists. "If you take it all as gospel, you are faced with a lot of internal contradictions."

Belsky agreed with Vaughn, but Christensen believed that Westman had identified an important cultural phenomenon: "the scientist as oracle." He noted how *profession* had shifted in meaning from "declaration of religious faith" to "career choice," arguing that the shift reveals a "troublesome" realignment in culture.

Closing out the first session of the consultation, Carlson remarked upon the growing prominence of statistical research as "the final arbiter of truth claims" in modern America. Given the cultural significance of their findings, researchers cannot dodge all responsibility by claiming that they are "just objective social scientists." Objective research on day care may be possible, but determining the implications of that research remains "one of the most heated domestic policy issues" in the United States. Carlson was particularly intrigued by Belsky's "Hegelian" conjecture about the historical appropriateness of the day-care center as an institution for "shaping individuals of maximum utility."

Burton White opened the second session of the consultation by sharing some radio tapes and posters used in California in the early 1980's as part of a campaign to encourage people to stay home and raise their own children. He noted that response to this campaign had varied widely, with some parents "fiercely supportive" of day care, some parents deeply committed to maternal care, and some parents simply confused.

Trying to address the practical issues, Westman reminded participants that the day-care debate could easily be distorted by the pressures of a supply-and-demand economy. Already he noted, day care has grown into a multi-billion dollar industry.

White interrupted to discount any notion that day-care providers would garner sizable profits caring for infants. He recounted Kinder Care's unsuccessful attempt to make sizable profits through infant day care. Except for fly-by-night operators, profits are held quite low by state regulations governing the permissible ratio of infants to caregivers.

Although Westman was reassured somewhat by this report, he noted that state legislatures are under pressure from day-care providers to increase the permissible ratio of infants and children to caregivers. Taking a broader assessment of the economic context of day care, he spoke of the widespread pain and despair among young people who are discovering how hard they must now work "to maintain the lifestyle that in the past could be maintained on a single average income."

Belsky intervened with the research of Robert Rector disproving the popular notion that "you need two wage earners to maintain what used to be maintained by one wage earner." Rather, what has happened is that material expectations rose: "TV was once a rare commodity. . . . But in the 80's everybody and his mother expects to have at least one VCR and maybe another to boot."

Westman conceded the point, but argued that parents still fall in two categories: 1) those who must struggle simply to survive; 2) those who work feverishly to meet raised levels of expectations. The pursuit of affluence is fostered by "quality of life" evaluations focused narrowly on the Gross National Product, unemployment, and household income. A truer assessment of the quality of life would clarify why so many people are "rushing around going nowhere, having no time for leisure." It is this hectic pace of modern life which denies parents the time to raise their own children. Few parents actually are delighted at putting their children in day care. Rather, they are "doing the best they can" to cope with the pain and pressures of their lives. The need for "psychological defenses" against this pain accounts for parental craving for reassurances about the quality of day care. These psychological defenses cause many parents to abdicate responsibility for child care and angrily insist that "somebody else has to solve this problem."

Still, Westman remained "quite optimistic" about the future. Drawing upon the work of futurists whose focus is social not technological, he predicted more introspection among Americans increasingly concerned about "a life that has meaning and purpose." To foster this social evolution, Westman called for more attention to "cultural values and long-term objectives." He stressed the lasting importance of good parenting and the high social costs of "incompetent parenting." Citing his recent research at the University of Wisconsin, he put "the cost of incompetent parenting" to society at "between $300,000 and $1.2 million per individual," depending on the degree to which public funds and facilities were utilized before the person entered the penal system. "Because society really depends upon the development of competent, responsible, productive, and compassionate citizens . . . what happens during the child's first three years is everyone's business." Westman pointed to the lessons learned from Headstart programs as useful models of how to help disadvantaged parents with young children. While expressing a preference for programs that work with the mother-child unit, Westman endorsed the termination of parental rights for those manifestly unfit for childrearing.

Exercising a chairman's prerogative, Carlson turned the discussion back to the relationship between social science and public policy, labelling that issue "critically important."

Belsky responded by arguing that while "a bridge" can be built between science and policy, those crossing that bridge must clearly distinguish between the two. Social science may generate information and evidence, but in a democracy we are all free to "take the information as we see it and do with it as we wish" in debating policy. Presuming that social science necessarily leads to this or that policy can lead to "a certain self-righteousness" or "hubris."

White offered a different perspective. He anticipated an "extraordinary shaping role" for social science if its practitioners could lobby for "the most powerful and the most conservative position" based on the agreed-upon evidence. As an example of how informed expertise can shape public policy, he cited the almost universal practice of delaying public instruction in literacy until a child is 5 or 6. He warned that unless social scientists do not try to influence the public debate on other issues (such as day care), "other forces will determine what we do."

Vaughn quarreled with White's historical example, arguing that while cognitive science might have confirmed the wisdom of delaying literacy instruction until age 6, the original justification lay in sources such as the Catholic doctrine defining the "age of reason."

Belsky raised a more fundamental objection, questioning whether even the best intentioned researchers would not "sift" the available data differently, arriving at "very different policy implications because of the relative weight they give things."

White felt things had drifted too far toward a pure relativism. Defending the possibility of reasoned agreement leading to clear policy implications, he pointed to the strong evidence implicating day-care centers in the spread of infectious diseases. "There is something you can hang your hat on."

Belsky did not hang his hat. After all, he countered, a number of studies of childhood diseases have identified the chief culprit as poor hygiene not nonmaternal care. So all of a sudden the issue is not day care but handwashing. More critically, researchers still remain uncertain both about the effects of day care upon children's immune systems and about the possible costs or benefits of such effects. Besides, the latest epidemiological study that Belsky had read found that day care accounts for a small part of the variance in respiratory diseases. This might be too big if it is your child who contracts infection at the day-care center, but such a statistic leads to no inevitable policy consensus.

Frustrated, White asked if we are then to conclude that research has "nothing to bring to these policy discussions." On the contrary, Belsky insisted that researchers have "a lot to bring to the discussions." But since empirical findings can be interpreted so many different ways, researchers should not be expected to dictate policy, "except as citizens like everybody else." Different people will put a "different spin" on the same set of data depending upon how they weigh the value of family vs. gender equality, the value of economic return vs. love and nurturing for children. Rather than looking to science to resolve these tensions, we need also to consult history, literature, and the humanities. Science, like these other disciplines, should contribute to policy deliberations and decisions, not dictate them.

Vaughn cast things in a different light by proposing that the role of researcher was not that of shaping official policy but rather that of providing parents with information so that they can make intelligent choices.

White persisted in his belief that research "feeds into" the policy-making process.

As one drawn into that process through his recent work on day care, Belsky could not resist a cynical metaphor: "Social scientists . . . risk becoming the prostitutes of policymakers; we are slept with when there is desire and are kicked out of bed when there is no longer interest." Researchers are hopelessly naive if they suppose that policymakers are all "open-minded, reasonable people who are willing to be right and willing to be wrong." As representatives of vested interests, policymakers are quite willing to stitch together this bit of developmental psychology, that piece of biology, that snippet of historical observation—all to serve their cause. Researchers must be "very alert" to the operation of these hidden agendas.

Trying to focus the discussion on a specific question, Carlson asked whether any research on day care had yet established "why parents do what they do."

Belsky acknowledged that while there is "a decent emerging literature" on some aspects of parent-child relations, the work on day-care placement has so far only looked at the factors of interest to economists and sociologists—such things as income and religiosity. The social psychology of day-care placement has yet to be investigated.

Despite the vacuum in research, Westman reported that psychiatrists are learning a fair amount about the question through clinical experience. Clinicians are seeing some parents who place their children in day care because of peer pressure. "There was a time when to work was to be guilty of neglecting a child. Now it is very clear that many women are working simply because they feel they are not fulfilled if they don't." On the other hand, some mothers use day care because to be at home with children in "a suburban kind of atmosphere . . . is a demanding and frustrating experience." Westman perceived a need for education that will "highlight parenting as a job," a career in which young adults can accomplish "something really worthwhile." Parents can be teachers and caregivers who "really provide something that no one else can for their child."

In skeptical reply, Belsky observed, "I don't see anybody buying that message, and I wonder if that's why it's not being sold." Contemporary Americans need to hear a message "more general than parenting"; they need to learn "the generic value of relationships." Americans need, too, to be reminded of "the bankrupt successes of life," typified by the man "who has got everything and fulfilled his dreams and is still an empty shell of a person." Invoking Abraham Maslow's "higher-order needs, of the original needs of men really," Belsky underscored the need for Americans to transcend "the pursuit of materialistic goods." "Until that message creeps back into our society . . . presentations about the importance of parenting won't have a fertile soil in which to grow."

This sounded too pessimistic for White, who recalled how once Head Start led to Sesame Street, middle-class interest in pre-school learning grew. Between 1968 and '78, the same period that witnessed the rise of nonparental child care, an increasing number of people began taking parenting seriously. As tangible evidence of this trend, White pointed to the proliferation of new books on how to raise a child. Likewise, toy stores sell an increasing number of toys designed to promote early childhood development. The evidence therefore suggests a marked divergence in cultural patterns: as some Americans were devaluing parenting, others were esteeming it more highly, so separating parents into two quite different types.

Unpersuaded, Belsky complained that the parenting books mentioned by White are all about "what goes on between the ears." "They are books of cognitive stimulation, raising the smarter, brighter, faster [child]." Such books are properly interpreted as part of "the hothouse effect," not as genuine appreciation of parenthood. What Americans need—and are not taught in these books—is the importance of "intimacy, closeness, emotion." Because they never learn this lesson, many "successful" Americans enjoy every consumer luxury while degenerating into "dead souls" in their emotional lives.

At this, Vaughn remarked that "the majority of rich people are pretty happy, and the majority of poor people aren't." Undeterred, Belsky cited survey research showing that except for those living in "extreme poverty," money doesn't make much difference in determining happiness. Happiness springs from "closeness" and "sharing emotions with others," things that cut across social class.

Calling a halt to the idealistic theorizing, White asked if there isn't something productive and useful that might be done, because "turning us into a humanistic society isn't going to be done soon."

Cautioning against despair, Belsky held out hope that parenting education of the sort developed by Berry Brazelton can make a significant and lasting difference in the way parents treat their children.

Carlson demurred on this point, wondering if programs in "parent education" were not dubiously contrived substitutes "for the way people used to learn how to be parents, which was by watching their own parents." Vaughn agreed that "people do acquire their child-rearing practices from being reared by their parents," but maintained that this process continues, even for kids cared for by someone other than parents. White confessed himself "suspicious of that kind of statement, because you are raising your own children anywhere from 18 to 30 years after you were raised." In his view, "what happens with most people is that when they have got the baby, they look around for some information," usually acquired from books, child-birth classes, or various "slices of society."

Vaughn still found it remarkable how many people "seem to find things in their parents that were in their own childhood." When White faulted Vaughn for his use of subjective and anecdotal evidence, Belsky entered the fray, citing research showing an intergenerational pattern in parenting styles and in parent-child bonding. He criticized White for his faith in the "informational basis of people's parenting" and for his doubts about the affective intuitive roots of parenting behavior. Personal background is important, he insisted: "I don't think we read a book and immediately abandon our affective systems."

White agreed that "fundamental differences" separated him from Belsky. Nor did he hold out much hope for resolving those differences with the "precious little data" currently available on what parents actually do with their children. Researchers needed to do much more direct observation of parents, he urged.

Belsky contended that the data on parental behavior was not so scanty as White supposed.

Sidestepping the empirical question, Christensen returned to the problems raised by "parent education" of a sort that substitutes a credentialed teacher for a parent. He questioned the assumption that there is "a natural community of interests between teachers and parents." "In our culture," he observed, "parents are often daunted and feel like their status is undermined by a whole bunch of people out there with paper credentials, with professional societies." An overweening faith in education can also lead to "the myth of the clean, well-lighted place," the belief that "everything important can be put on display with lights under and on top of it." Pedagogues often forget that life is "full of ambiguities, family life particularly." These ambiguities are exacerbated by the plurality of lifestyles in America.

Since it is impossible to run a scientific study to determine how people *should* live their family lives, policymakers should be careful not to enact day-care policies that subsidize one lifestyle choice at the expense of another.

Barglow took this as his cue to read from a recent statement from the U.S. Chamber of Commerce urging the Federal Government to "resist the temptation to mandate specific employee benefits, to regulate industry, or subsidize or compete with the private sector in day care or to impose a costly and monolithic Federal child-care program."

Belsky was "disgusted" by clichéd conservative references to "monolithic this and monolithic that." He criticized this kind of straw-man rhetoric as one of the weaknesses of conservative lobbying against the Federal ABC Bill on day care. In practice, no program is monolithic, he asserted.

Even if the program is not monolithic, Barglow asked whether government should provide "the main solution" to the problems Americans have created by not devoting enough attention and love to their children.

In answer, Blum endorsed Federally mandated parental leave, despite the objections of the Chamber of Commerce.

Can social science tell us, Carlson asked, whether parental leave is the best policy option available?

Vaughn reiterated his view that the social scientists' task is simply to "present information to people," preferably the general public rather than just legislators. The people then can shape their own policies.

Signaling to all present that he was "crossing the bridge" from science to value preferences, Belsky declared himself solidly in favor of parental leave. He accused conservatives of "a real serious inconsistency" when they refuse to support parental leave at the same time that they champion tax credits to give parents freedom to stay home.

Rising to defend conservatives, Christensen argued that parental leave does impose costs on business, costs that are passed along in various ways to traditional families, thus creating a kind of hidden subsidy. "The traditional family ends up paying for someone else's life-style choice."

Belsky parried this criticism by arguing that since virtually all women are in the work force until bearing a first child, parental leave is not a benefit that subsidizes only one group of people. Besides, he urged, the hidden-subsidy argument should not be persuasive for any community-minded person. Those who use the hidden-subsidy argument are in effect saying, "If I'm not getting a benefit, then nobody else is either." Not only does this way of thinking violate "the very notion of community," it is also very short-sighted since children reared in traditional homes must eventually deal at school and elsewhere with children raised in other types of homes.

Still a voice for "the grievances of conservatives," Christensen decried the emergence of a statist morality which allows Americans "to live an alternate life-style on every day but April 15th." Tax day has become the nation's only "immovable feast," as the state does more and more of what families used to do, making the tax burden grow larger and larger. He alleged that this arrangement places unfair burdens on those who do not need state services because they have maintained their family through sacrifice and commitment. Such people end up paying part of the tax burden imposed by casual divorce and family dissolution. It galls conservatives, he said, that the same government officials who dismiss morality as simply a matter of personal preference are then quite willing to impose the costs of moral dissolution through higher taxes.

Ideological disputes did not interest White, who wished to return to the question of how research could guide educational policy. Such research, he noted, had shown that serious academic difficulty lies ahead for a six-year-old who is a year or more behind in language and intelligence. Such research had also demonstrated that similar problems lie ahead of a three-year-old who is nine months or more behind in language and intelligence. Nor have programs like Headstart generally succeeded in turning slow three-year-olds into ready six-year-olds. "If the country wants to have an intelligent educational system, it ought to do something to prevent the build up of a deficit in a three-year-old."

As an example of an initiative that aims to prevent such early learning deficits, White pointed to a program in Missouri for parent training and support. Based upon intense study of the families of especially well-developed three-year-olds, this program reaches out to parents from their local elementary school to help raise children who are secure, socially at ease, and well-developed in language and intelligence. This program not only sends out a training unit to the home, but it also introduces young parents to other young parents. This program assures parents that if any problems develop during their child's first years, they will receive speedy assistance.

Belsky cited new research substantiating the positive long-term effects of parent-child programs in reducing behavioral problems, truancy and social dysfunction, but he cautioned that such initiatives are "remarkably expensive."

Neither White nor Westman viewed financing as an insuperable obstacle. White saw the Missouri program as a model that kept costs down by relying on parental involvement, while Westman noted that in any case the parent-education programs were less expensive than day care. Blum, however, did not want cost comparisons used to justify either/or choices between day care and parent education. Nor was she happy with Christensen's previous reference to day care as a "life-style issue." The question of "working mothers" lies at "the heart of our society and our economy," she insisted.

When Carlson suggested that parental choices vary depending upon social class, Belsky elaborated by citing statistics showing that many poor mothers have always had to work. The dramatic growth in maternal employment in the last decade has shown up among middle-class mothers, "the people who previously had a choice," but who now feel either economic or cultural pressure to work.

Blum and Westman both endorsed the government's obligation to help poorer households meet their child-care needs, but Christensen was wary of state regulation. Isn't it odd, he asked, that the very people who insist that a woman should have absolute life-or-death control over the child until birth—a control not even legally shared with a husband—are the same people who will not trust mothers to arrange their own child care without state regulation? "If there is a consistency in those two positions, it is that both undermine traditional family authority."

Shifting the focus from politics to research, Carlson asked whether any consensus was emerging on the risks of day care.

Belsky answered that the cumulative research does appear to identify a "window of vulnerability" for infants placed in nonparental care extensively during the first year of life. Other research shows that there is "no apparent risk" for three, four, and five-year-olds in quality day care. He emphasized that since relatively few working mothers (only about 15 percent) use center-based care, the term "day care" is often applied to many types of non-parental arrangements. He stressed that the data base is not yet "rich enough" for social scientists to make many sweeping pronouncements on the effects of day care, particularly quality day care. Nor did he think it fair that many people were interpreting his own work as evidence that "day care is all bad; all day care is bad." White thought the proper question was not whether day care posed risks, but whether day care is "the very best way to raise a child." Admitting that quality day care offers advantages over family life in some households, he could not see any convincing evidence that day care is actually preferable to parental care for most children. Belsky did note that some research suggests that children in preschool from middle-class homes do develop better social skills than children who have been exclusively at home. But White did not put much stock in these studies, arguing that in studies done before the early 1960's researchers could find nothing to indicate that "a child from a solid home suffered any disadvantage from never having gone to nursery care."

Carlson responded to the notion that day care teaches social skills in a different way, returning to Belsky's previous conjecture that day care fosters a "false self" or "a new personality type."

Belsky was not ready to give "a firm statement." Yet he speculated that "the notion of a false self" might explain the pattern of avoidance, noncompliance, and aggression seen in preschoolers placed in nonparental care for 20 or more hours per week during the first year of life. Such children may be learning "not to express their distress" at being left by their parents. Although they may act "superficially compliant," they may actually become deeply noncompliant "because they don't accept direct tuition from adults" because they have learned that adults "aren't so special." Having been schooled in a sort of "impression management" approach to social relationships, such children may start developing "a manipulative type character."

Although Westman saw clinical evidence to support Belsky's conjecture, Barglow complained of a "relative paucity of data." Until more long-term research was completed, he saw no reason to posit a link between day care and the development of a "false self."

Belsky conceded that the research is "open to multiple interpretations." "The data is such a mess that it is exceedingly easy to stir it up and say there is nothing going on," he remarked. Even if it is acknowledged that there is a link between day care and emotional problems, no "causal mechanisms" have yet been clearly identified. Still, Belsky was struck by the number of people who tell him that their own work points to some kind of linkage, even if they are "not willing to stand up and say it."

Westman complained that in most studies of the effects of day care, the assessment is from some point of view other than the child's. Westman then asked Belsky and Vaughn what advice they would give a mother with a baby or a toddler who could either care for her own child or go to work and place the child in institutional day care. When both Belsky and Vaughn said that the decision should hinge upon the desire of the mother, Westman complained that they were still focusing on the parent, not the needs of the child. He was disappointed at not hearing an affirmation of the "social value" of caring for one's child.

Belsky saw matters differently. He thought that a mother would be making "a serious mistake" if she placed her baby in day care if she personally wanted to care for her own child and was economically able to do so. On the other hand, if a mother either did not want to or could not afford to stay home, he failed to see why some other person could not satisfy the baby's need for an enduring bond to a caregiver. When Christensen questioned the possibility of "paying someone to love a child," Belsky countered that "there are other people besides parents who can love children well," even if they are paid. Acknowledging a biological predisposition to love our own children, Belsky pointed to adoption as prime evidence that it is possible to love other people's children, too.

Himself an adoptive father, Christensen would not accept the comparison between adoption and day care, since adoption entails a lifetime commitment, not the short-term employment characteristics of day care. Belsky admitted that length of commitment is a critical variable for evaluating child care and that in an ideal arrangement the same person serves as caregiver for three to five years. As the length of the caregiver's commitment declines, reasons for concern grow. Nor is it possible to receive "a developmental dispensation" justifying frequent changes in caregivers so long as other aspects of the care are of high quality. Yet Belsky remained optimistic that when working mothers rely on a grandmother or a neighbor, enduring bonds can develop between caregiver and child. "Kids have been reared like that for eons," he concluded.

Barglow felt that the discussion of the risks of nonparental care would be unbalanced unless it was recognized that in "a significant percentage" of homes the children would "be better off *not* being taken care of by their own mothers and fathers."

Belsky conceded the existence of depressed, desperate, and otherwise unfit parents, but he expressed unease at the judgment that "a significant portion of the population are not good enough caregivers for their own kids." Christensen had scarcely voiced concurring fears when White raised the ante with the prediction that "within fifty years or perhaps less there will be licensing for parents."

Carlson reminded those present that the idea that the state should intervene in the home for "the best interests of the child" is a historical novelty. He reminded participants that before roughly 1900, American social thought centered on "what is best for the family or what is best for the lineage. . . . This child-centered focus is really a product of the late 19th century and of the 20th century." To ask "what is best for the child—as social scientists now routinely do—is already to accept a set of assumptions about what *best* means." Carlson wondered if the very way we ask social science questions does not "invariably lead us towards that focus on the individual," and away from a concern for the family and larger community.

In this vein, Belsky remarked that many sociobiologists have perceived conflicts of interest between parents and children, analogous to the conflicts of interest that crop up between communities and nations. He acknowledged that relatively few people want to argue with the popular notion (found in the earlier version of Westman's paper) that what is best for the child is also best for the family and society, but he criticized such views as "platitudes," which are "too convenient."

White admitted the possibility of conflicts of interest, but he saw more than a platitude in Westman's "strong stand" in affirming that "society in the future depends on the caliber of the individuals we have today."

Belsky still worried that a concern for society's future could easily become a "cost-benefit analysis that may depersonalize children." Aren't the smiles of children today, at this moment, valuable in their own right? Why doesn't that matter any more? Such questions moved Belsky to reflect on the 1950's when mothers stayed home with their children not necessarily because it built character but "because it made their children feel better. . . . There was a sort of giving without an expectation of return."

Vaughn did not want to go too far in following children's preferences. After all, he cautioned, "children make a lot of mistakes about what is good for them. . . . That is why we lock the medicine cabinet." Adults must bear responsibility for guiding children, sometimes against their desires.

For Christensen, the issue still remained of whether those guiding adults should be parents or someone else. In particular, he questioned the desirability of foreign models for child care, such as those found in Sweden, Denmark, or West Germany. Those who hold up such models for imitation seem strangely indifferent to the depressed fertility and high illegitimacy rates in such lands. Could it be, he wondered, that the appearance of a particularly good day-care system or a particularly extensive set of state services actually signals a retreat from family life and not a real concern for children?

For a different foreign perspective, Westman turned to Israel. In the kibbutzim, the Israelis developed perhaps the best controlled study of collective child-rearing yet undertaken, motivated by a desire to achieve equality for women. But now, the kibbutzim have largely backed away from institutional care for infants and have gone back to the nuclear family. The feeling responsible for this shift in Israel is now increasingly evident in America. "That feeling is one of parental guilt, worry, and anxiety."

Belsky complained that a surprising number of people— including many scientists—have criticized him for publishing findings that foster guilt. Belsky further ventured his personal opinion that "guilt is a good thing," something that keeps people on their toes. He conjectured that it may be the mothers who aren't feeling guilty who are most likely to see avoidance behavior in their children. "I'm more concerned with [guilt] prematurely going away than staying."

Although a few participants wanted to debate the beneficence of guilt, Carlson wanted to return to the foreign scene. Does the Israeli experience have any relevance to American circumstances?

Belsky interpreted the Israeli experience as evidence that if parents in this country were given a free choice, most would care for their own babies. The Israelis discovered—for biological and other reasons—that they wanted to care for their own children. Most Americans would make a similar choice, if they could. For many people, the ideal option would be to care for their baby full time for 6 months or a year, then work part time as they return to work on a gradual basis.

Vaughn suspected that almost every communal experiment has failed over time because of biological impulses that predispose people to care more for their own children. Belsky agreed that biology and emotion both motivate parents to see that their children are well cared for.

Not at all sure that biology was guiding parents aright, White saw a great many middle-class parents placing their children in day care without knowing the pros and cons of such a decision. He hypothesized that a "monkey see, monkey do" mentality was at work, as young couples mindlessly imitate what they see others doing. He reaffirmed his support for programs that will educate parents in their responsibilities.

Belsky again marveled at how quickly the employment rate for mothers of infants had risen, noting a 45 percent growth in employment for this group of women between 1978 and 1984. Although he agreed with White that this pattern reflected "monkey see, monkey do" behavior, Belsky detected a deeper problem. He cited Jimmy Carter's "malaise speech" as a telling diagnosis of a widespread "sense of being lost." Americans who feel lost for a sense of purpose and direction are likely to "do what everybody else is doing."

Vaughn found it somewhat misleading to speak of a dramatic shift in the employment rate of the mothers of infants. Most of the mothers in question are not having a baby and *then* deciding to work. Rather, most of these women are already in the labor force *before* their pregnancy. Staying out of the work force for an extended period to have a baby means a serious reduction in their accustomed income.

Nor are a mother's costs for withdrawing from the workforce merely economic, Belsky stressed. American culture has shifted dramatically against the mother who stays at home. When she says, "I'm staying home with my baby," others say, "But what are you *really* doing?" The at-home mother has become "a voiceless soul" in contemporary America, consigned to the same cultural oblivion as the working mother of the 1950's.

Barglow returned to the more practical question of whether a mother should return to the work force quickly after the birth of a child or delay her return for a year or more. He puzzled over the advice of Sandra Scarr, who has recommended that to avoid problems mothers should return to work early, "when the child can't complain very much."

Such advice grated on Belsky, who interpreted it as "the old avoidance of feelings." It is true that a mother going back to work when her child is 13, 14, or 18 months old will face "a much more distressed baby" than if she re-enters the workforce shortly after the child's birth. But the real question is, Do you have a short-term gain and a long-term cost? If the mother returns to work quickly, will she undermine "the relationship base" vital to the child's emotional development?

Shifting gears, Belsky thought it important in a gathering like this one to assess available public policies on child care. He endorsed policy options that would foster flexibility and free choice at a time when most mothers "don't fit quite in either the pattern of June Cleaver in the 1950's or the career woman in the late 1970's." He thought it a mistake to pit the Bush policy of tax credits against the

ABC policy of day-care subsidy, since both ideas "have merit." Nor could he see why those who support tax credits for young families should not also support parental leave. In this analysis, the ABC Bill for day care holds benefits even for traditional families, since "people who do put their kids in care are going to punish us all if their kids are in lousy care." ABC would help attract qualified people to day care, so reducing the likelihood of bad care.

Blum went on record firmly in support of parental leave and of changes in the workplace offering more flexible options for women. She found it remarkable that young employees now often work a brutal schedule of 60 to 80 hours a week. How can this be, she wondered, given that just twenty years ago many people were anticipating the adoption of a four-day work week? Perhaps the explanation is that now that women finally proved that they can do whatever men can do, men have determined that in order to show their superiority they must work hours that are impossible for women with families.

In his policy summation, White endorsed programs designed to make it possible for every newborn to be cared for full-time by either a parent or grandparent during the first 6 months and to spend the majority of their waking hours during the next two years with one of those six people. Second, White called for a Federally mandated floor on welfare benefits for single mothers so that they can care for their own children.

Barglow advocated more government spending on research projects, especially longitudinal studies needed to resolve differences of opinion expressed at this consultation.

Westman did not want anyone to forget the very small segment of the population comprising high risk children and high risk parents. Such people need intensive help and intervention. Indeed, the problems created in such households justify the notion of licensing parents, he asserted.

The idea of licensing parents provoked strenuous opposition from Christensen, who warned: "That way lies 'Big Brother.'" He opined that in a country that is religiously and culturally diverse, all family policies must respect that diversity by avoiding anything that smacks of life-style engineering. Government policy should rest upon a strong presumption in favor of parental authority, a presumption laid aside only in cases where parents are doing things very clearly harmful to the child.

Seeking to allay Christensen's fears, Westman specified that only an extremely small fraction of American parents would fail the standards he had in mind.

Attention next shifted to state licensing of day care rather than of parents. Barglow hoped that government could "do better," especially in reducing the ratio of infants to caregivers. But White looked back over fifteen years of child-care regulations and saw more reason for despair than hope. Belsky appeared to split the difference between the two by supporting the regulation of public facilities while questioning the feasibility of regulating all child-care arrangements. He faulted the conservative argument against any regulation by pointing to existing regulations on automobiles and water. "Why don't children and families deserve the same protection?" he asked. On the other hand, if the state tried to legislate all child-care arrangements, it would end up issuing "licenses to neglect," unwittingly making the state an accomplice in offenses committed against children. Ending with an analogy, Belsky reasoned that anybody can drive around a home-built car in his own backyard, but he can't take it out on a public road.

Satisfied that all had spoken their minds, Carlson adjourned the consultation, hoping that the proceedings had opened new questions and stimulated new thinking among those present.

Day Care: Changing Incentives

by James R. Walker

Introduction

C hild care has become a leading domestic public policy issue. Since the 1988 presidential campaign, rarely has a month passed without some media attention given to a facet of the policy debate concerning day care. Two trends motivate much of the policy discussion. First, an increasing proportion of married women with young children participate in the labor market. During the period 1970 to 1985, the proportion of married women participating in the labor market with preschool children approximately doubled, increasing from 26 percent to 51 percent (Hayghe 1988). Second, an increasing proportion of preschool children receive out-of-home nonrelative care. In 1965, 62 percent of preschool children with working mothers received in-home relative care whereas only 24 percent of such children received out-of-home care. By 1985, the proportion of children receiving each type of care was nearly equal: 48 percent in relative care and 45 percent in out-of-home care (Hofferth 1988).

This paper presents a simple economic framework for understanding these trends. The framework presented in section 2.0 is an example of household production which recognizes that child care can be produced in the household or purchased in the market (day care). Thus household decisions on the use of day care have aspects of both production and consumption. In fact, an important feature of the model of household production is the derivation of the appropriate "price of child care" produced in the household. These prices, along with other prices, resources and preferences of the household determine the usage of day care. An important insight of this approach is that female labor supply and child care decisions are *jointly* determined within the household; both choices depend on the same determinants and hence are mutually dependent. Causality runs from exogenous factors, such as wages, product prices, household endowments and technology to labor supply and child care; causality does not run between labor supply and child care.

Empirical evidence on the changing incentives for the use of day care is presented in Section 3.0. From the analytical framework of Section 2.0 the incentives are categorized as affecting either the work/no work decision or the choice of child care mode. The empirical evidence suggests that incentives affecting both choices have changed during the past fifteen years.

Within the Reagan policy of privatization and decentralization of social services (Kahn and Kammerman 1987), many policy advocates have called upon private corporations to accept a more active role in expanding the provision of day care. The fourth section of the paper reviews the changing corporate incentives in the supply and use of day care. A conclusion presented in this section is that the incentives have not changed substantially to induce corporations to change their provision of day care. Individual households will continue to assume the primary role in changing the child-care landscape, now and in the immediate future. The paper concludes with a summary.

2.0 *An Economic Framework of the Demand for Child Care*

This section exposits a simple economic framework of consumer choice to highlight the relevant factors that determine day care usage by individuals. This framework is an example of household production in that child care can be produced in the household or purchased in the market (day care). The framework thus integrates the theory of the consumer and the theory of the firm. Integration of production and consumption aspects of behavior occurs in a two-step procedure. In the first step, production aspects of behavior are used to determine the appropriate price of child care produced in the household as well as the value of time used to produce that care. The second step uses standard consumer theory to determine these "shadow" prices and other prices, which along with household resources and preferences determine the household's consumption of each product.

Subsection 2.1 describes the basic framework of a household production model, including the determination of the price of child care and the value of time used in the household. Subsection 2.2 presents the various mechanisms through which changing economic and policy environments affect the household's incentives for using day care. Subsection 2.3 extends the basic framework to enhance its usefulness for understanding the empirical evidence presented in section 3.0.

2.1 *A Household Production Model*

Child care has aspects of both a service and a product. Clearly, it is an activity which is time intensive, and particularly female time intensive. In order for a woman with a small child to work in the labor market, custodial child care must be arranged. By this perspective child care is a service. This has been the perspective of most economic models of female labor supply (Heckman 1974). While many of the tasks associated with child care are mundane and unenjoyable, other tasks and interactions with children are enjoyable. These aspects make child care an economic "good"—a source of satisfaction to the household. By this perspective child care is a consumption activity; through child care the household consumes "child services" which are valued by the household. This is the perspective of neoclassical models of fertility (Becker 1960). The perspective of this paper combines these two views by assuming that households value the quality of their children and that child care is a time-intensive activity which affects child quality. This synthesis is achieved by defining day care to be all forms of nonparental child care. This perspective then provides two, perhaps conflicting, motivations for the use of day care: (1) as a custodial service while the woman is at work and (2) as an activity affecting child quality. The exposition of the framework is easier if we separate the two motivations. In this subsection, day care is only custodial, having no affect on child quality. The potential effect of day care on child quality is incorporated into the framework in subsection 2.3.

The presentation begins with a description of the consumer's choice problem. Assume that parents value the quality of their children, denoted as Q, and a composite consumption commodity, Z, that includes all nonchild sources of satisfaction. To simplify the discussion, assume that the number of children is fixed. Preferences of the household determine the subjective valuation of Q and Z. Following standard neoclassical theory, we assume that the household seeks to maximize utility obtained from the consumption of Q and Z.

The resources available to the household limit consumption. For example, the household's budget constraint (purchases cannot exceed income) limits market expenditures. Another constraint is the production of child quality within the household. As stated above, assume that child quality is determined only within the household; child care (day care) received outside of the household is purely custodial. Child quality can be produced in the household by combining market goods, X, and mother's time, t. Recognizing that women provide most of the child care within the household, we assume that only mother's time can be used to produce child quality.[1] Higher quality care is synonymous with higher child quality. Greater inputs of mother's time and market goods yield higher child quality and hence, higher quality care is more expensive. The father's role in the household (even if present) is passive. The man is productive in the market and not in the household and therefore contributes income to the household. He does not contribute to the production of Q. The woman may also work in the labor market and receive a fixed hourly wage. Custodial day care must be purchased for the time spent in the market by the woman. The woman's net wage rate is the market wage less the hourly cost of day care.

The novel aspect of household production models is the representation of the household as both a consumer and a producer. The household must decide not only how much Q and Z to consume, it must also decide the best combination of mother's time and market goods to use in the production of Q. How does the household solve these problems? Subject to its income, household technology, the price of all commodities and its preferences, the household determines the optimal combination of Q and Z. The price of the composite commodity is set in the market. The price of child quality is determined by the household by its activity as a producer. As a producer, the household will produce Q according to the available household technology in the least-cost fashion. The price of Q so determined is called a shadow price, since it is determined within the household and not in the market. Shadow prices are central to the analysis. In what follows, we consider the production aspects of the household's decision problem and the determination of the shadow price of child quality.

Analogous to a cake recipe, technology is the detailed description of how inputs are combined to produce output, Q. For example, assume that to produce a unit of child quality requires exactly α units of the mother's time, t, and exactly β units of market good X. Mathematically, this fixed-proportion technology[2] is represented as:

(1) $Q = MIN(t/\alpha, X/\beta)$.

In words, output Q is the minimum of two ratios, t/α and X/β. For example, if more than α units of time are used but only β units of the market good X are purchased, then output does not increase but still equals one. Since no additional output is produced unless both inputs are increased, efficient production occurs when time and goods are used in the fixed proportion α/β.[3]

What is the cost of child quality produced under this fixed-proportion technology? Assume that the woman works in the labor market at net wage $\overline{W}$ (net of the cost of custodial day care) and that the price of X is P_x. Denote the unit cost of child quality as π. One unit of Q requires α units of the woman's time, costing $\alpha\overline{W}$ and β units of the market good costing of βP_x. The total cost of a unit of child quality is the sum of the time cost and cost of goods:

(2) $\pi = \alpha \overline{W} + \beta P_x$.

Clearly, cost is independent of output level so that each unit of child quality costs π to produce.[4] The total cost of producing Q units of child quality is πQ. The household must not incur a loss in the production of Q, hence, "revenue" equals πQ. For all levels of output, shadow price equals unit cost; that is, shadow price also equals π.

The fixed-proportion technology illustrates the determination of the cost of child quality produced in the household. By equation (2), child quality is determined by technology (α, β) and market prices of inputs ($\overline{W}$, P_x). Notice, also from equation (2), an increase in the price of either time or market goods increases the cost of child quality. I will say more on this in the next section.

The derivation of equation (2) assumes that the woman participates in the labor market. This assumption provides a well defined price for the woman's time. What is the appropriate cost of time for a woman who does *not* participate in the market? In this case, her "shadow" wage is used. The value the woman assigns to her time is her shadow wage. For example, assume a woman earns $8/hour for each hour in the labor market, values another unit of leisure at $10/hour and can produce another unit of child quality, valued at $12/hour. The woman will produce child care until the incremental hour in child care equals the incremental value of leisure. In this example, because each hour of leisure is more highly valued than market work, the woman will not participate in the market. One can think of the shadow wage as the value associated with the woman's best use of an additional increment of time. The market wage is the price at which the woman can exchange her time for money in the labor market. A well known result from the neoclassical model of labor supply is indicated by this example—a woman *not* participating in the labor market has a shadow wage (or alternative use of time) which exceeds her market wage. Clearly, for a woman participating in the market, her shadow wage equals her market wage.

The concept of shadow prices is useful because the household uses these and regular market prices to determine the allocation of resources. The relevant price of child quality produced in the household is π, the relevant price of the woman's time is her shadow wage (which may or may not equal her market wage). To combine these observations, let W^* denote the woman's shadow wage, then (2) can be rewritten as equation (3):

(3) $\pi = \alpha W + \beta P_x$,

where,

> W, the market wage net of child care costs, if the woman works,

$W =$

> W^*, the shadow wage, if the woman does not work.

Hence, whether the woman works or not, the price of child quality produced in the household is given by equation (3).

There is one important distinction between shadow prices and market prices: market prices are exogenous (affect but are not affected by decisions of the household) while shadow prices are endogenous (determined by the actions of the household). The shadow wage will depend therefore on the same exogenous factors that determine the optimal allocation of time, the production of the household good and consumption of the composite commodity. Shadow prices will change when any of the exogenous variables change. To see this, consider the shadow wage of a woman who has just won a million dollar lottery. This (unexpected) windfall is an increase to the household's unearned income (one of the exogenous variables). By winning the lottery, the woman can use her new monetary resources to hire others to do many of the more mundane household chores (e.g., laundry, cleaning, cooking, etc.) normally associated with household production.[5] That is, having won the lottery permits the woman to substitute market goods for her time input into household production. To be willing to make this exchange, the woman must consider her time more valuable—her shadow wage rate has increased.

Finally, notice that the solution to the household decision problem determines an allocation of the woman's time between household production of child quality (child care) and market work. Hence, child quality, female labor supply and the use of day care are *jointly* determined by the household. These outcomes of the household choice process are mutually dependent and are determined by the same exogenous factors: market prices of all goods, including day care, household resources and technology. An important implication is that female labor-force participation is associated with the use of day care but market work *does not cause* the usage of day care. Nor does usage of day care cause female participation in the labor market. Rather, changing patterns in day care and female labor supply are caused by changes in one (or several) of the exogenous variables.

2.2 Changes in Household Behavior in Response to Changes in the Environment

To an economist, "changing incentives" means changes in exogenous variables. This subsection discusses how changes in prices, household resources and technology generate changes in the outcomes of the household's choice process: consumption levels of Z and Q, and the corresponding allocation of the woman's time between home and market production. The analytical framework afforded by the household production approach for understanding these mechanisms is the primary advantage of this approach. Unfortunately, the exposition of these effects is still difficult because the mechanisms are diverse and somewhat complicated. It will be useful for the reader to keep in mind the basic principles from the theory of demand: an increase in the resources of the household increases demand (more is preferred to less); an increase in price reduces demand for that good (demand curves are negatively sloped.) These principles will be applied repeatedly in the subsequent analysis.

2.2.1 *Incomes and Substitution Effects*

To begin, assume that the number of children is fixed and that child-care technology is given in equation (1) with the associated price of child quality in equation (3). For the moment, assume that the woman works in the market at a constant net hourly wage. Consider an increase in the household's property income. Resources of the household have unambiguously increased. By the principle that more is preferred to less, the demand for all goods increase; more of the composite commodity is consumed and child quality increases. Since household production of child quality requires mother's time, the woman reallocates more time to the production of child quality and less time to the market. Since the use of day care is purely custodial and directly linked to labor supply, an increase in household income that reduces labor supply also reduces the use of day care. Hence, increases in household income reduce the woman's labor supply and day-care usage while increasing the consumption of Z and child quality and child care produced in the household.

Now assume that prior to the increase in property income, the woman does *not* participate in the labor market. As before, increased income increases the demand of Z and Q. Unlike the preceding case, the increase in income does not leave all prices constant. By equation (3) the price of child quality depends on the woman's shadow wage. Moreover, by the lottery example, increases in household income increase the shadow wage. By this transmission mechanism, the price of child quality increases. Hence, by the second general principle (demand curves slope downward) less child quality will be demanded. This negative substitution effect (also called a price effect) mitigates and perhaps could dominate the positive income effect on the demand for child quality. A prediction of the economic framework is that the effect of an increase in property income on the demand for child quality should be larger for women working in the market than for women not working in the market. The net effect on the demand for child quality for nonworking women is, however, ambiguous.[6]

Consider now an increase in the woman's market wage rate. Each hour of the woman's time endowment is worth more; the woman can work fewer hours to achieve the same labor-market income, the income effect increases the demand for Z and Q. Moreover, since most households receive between 80-90 percent of their monetary resources through the labor market, income effects could be quite sizable. The income effect implies that female labor supply declines. However, there are substitution effects to consider. From equation (3), the price of child quality increases with an increase in the market wage. The household will substitute away from the higher priced good (substitute Z for Q), reducing its demand for Q. Less consumption of Q releases time from home production and this creates more time for labor market activity. Hence, the substitution effect of an increase in wages increases labor supply, use of day care and consumption of Z and decreases Q and parental child care. The net effect of the income and substitution effects on child quality and labor supply are ambiguous. Conventional wisdom from labor economics is that for women the substitution effect dominates the income effect, implying that an increase in the market wage increases female labor supply (Killingsworth 1983).

2.2.2 Technological Change

Another advantage of a household production approach is that it explicitly incorporates into the analysis the impact of household technological change on the choices of the household. Technological innovation has occurred in the household, just as it has elsewhere in our society. The contemporary household scarcely resembles the household of thirty years ago. Since 1960 many new household appliances have been introduced, for example, microwaves, food processors, self-cleaning ovens, and the myriad of small electrical kitchen appliances. Nor have all the innovations been confined to kitchen appliances, as other innovations include frozen food, permanent press clothes, fire-retardant children's clothes and disposable diapers.[7] Recent developments in microcomputers suggest that the rate of technical change in the household will not noticeably slacken in the near future.

Technological innovations have two important common elements that clearly affect household choices. First, innovation is equivalent to an increase in endowments of the household, thus one effect of technological change on the demand for goods is through an income effect. Second, innovations change the production process in the household. Many of the items listed above are labor-saving devices; less labor input is required for the same output.[8] Innovation permits a substitution of goods for time in the household. In other words, technological innovation changes the input requirements (α, β) for household production. Relative prices of household-produced goods also change.

To illustrate these effects, consider the fixed-proportion technology of equation (1). Assume that a change in household production occurs that reduces the time input α for goods produced in the household. A decline in α is equivalent to an increase in the time endowment.[9] An increase in an endowment is an income effect which has the impact of increasing the demand for all goods. The decline in α also induces a price effect as the cost of the household commodity is lower (confer equation (3)). The magnitude of the decline in cost depends directly on the share of product cost attributed to the time input $(\alpha W/\pi)$. In the presence of lower (relative and absolute) household prices, the household will substitute toward this good. Hence, both the price and income effects support an increase in the demand for the household good. Other changes to the input requirement set can be considered but will not be developed here.

2.2.3 Government Policy

The economic model also provides a natural approach for analyzing the effects of government policies and programs on household incentives. As should be clear, within this framework, the mechanisms by which government programs influence household decisions are through the effects on the household's budget constraint (i.e., prices, resources, and technology). Income taxes and most social programs directly affect the household's budget constraint. Any social program which changes the household's budget constraint will induce income and substitution effects on the household's choice outcomes. Potentially, every social program has the effect, whether intended or not, of changing the household's demand for day care. The usefulness of the approach depends on translating the proposed policy change into a change in the consumer's budget set. An example of how this is done is given below.

Let us consider the impact on the budget constraint of the dependent-care tax credit, a program intended to change the demand for day care. Every tax unit (household) may claim an income-tax credit for child-care expenditures on a dependent child. The size of the tax credit depends on the household's income and child-care expense. Families with total income of less than $10,000 may claim a tax credit of 30 percent of their child-care expenditures, up to a maximum expenditure of $2,400 for one child and $4,800 for two or more children. Child-care expenditure limits are the same for all income classes, though the credit percentage declines for incomes above $10,000. The percentage declines by 1 percentage point for each $2,000 of income above $10,000 up to $28,000. Households with total incomes greater than $28,000 may claim only 20 percent of their child-care expenses. The maximum tax credit is $720 (30 percent of $2,400) for one child and $1,440 (30 percent of $4,800) for two or more children. The tax credit is nonrefundable; the tax credit cannot exceed the tax liability of the household.

The impact of this tax credit on the budget constraint depends on the situation of the household. For a family with one child, spending more than $2,400, and having a tax liability greater than $720, the effect of the tax credit is to augment the household's income by the value of the credit. For this family, enactment of the tax credit produces only an income effect. Consider now the effect on a family that has a tax liability greater than $720 but which did not spend the allowable maximum on child care prior to the enactment of the law. For this family, additional day-care expenditures on child care up to $2,400 are subsidized by the government. Since the after-tax price of day care has declined, the household experiences both income and substitution effects. Finally, consider a family with no tax liability. Since the tax credit is nonrefundable, it has no value for this household. For the first two household types considered, income and substitution effects generated by the program influence household decision-making as outlined above.

The preceding analysis focused on the effect of a single program in isolation of other programs. Interaction among social programs change the magnitude of the effects obtained when programs are evaluated separately. For example, for a family with one child and income less than $10,000 the implied maximum value of the dependent child care tax credit is $720. Many low-income households also qualify for the earned income tax credit. For many of these families, the earned income tax credit eliminates any tax liability for the household. The value of the child care tax credit for these families is zero not $720.[10] This example highlights the fact that determination of the total effect on the budget constraint is neither simple nor straightforward. However, once the impact on the budget set has been determined, the consequences for the consumer's behavior are summarized by the implied income and substitution effects.

The preceding example considers a policy that directly affects the household's budget constraint. Some policies have indirect (and perhaps unintended) effects on the consumer's budget set. For example, government programs or policies legislated on suppliers affect the cost of day care. Most notable are licensing standards imposed by many localities on day-care center and family home providers. A change in the standards such as an increase in the staff/child ratio increases the supplier's cost. The increase in cost will be passed on to the consumer in the form of higher prices for child care. Equivalent to a decrease in the woman's market wage, an increased price of child care reduces the woman's net wage rate. The impact on the household's budget constraint, labor supply, and demand for child quality are, with a change in sign, as described for a change in the woman's wage. Other supply-based policies can be evaluated in the same way. As is evident, determining the implied effects on supplier's costs and the resulting market prices is a nontrivial task. However, regardless of who pays the tax or receives the subsidy (transfer payment), through the operation of the market, the consumer's budget constraint ultimately is changed.

2.3 Expanded Definitions of Child Welfare

The analysis of the preceding section assumed that out-of-home child care is purely custodial, neither adding nor subtracting to the child's quality. Much of the policy debate surrounding day care has in fact centered on the effect of day care on child development. This subsection discusses how such considerations can be incorporated into the analysis. This discussion naturally leads to an expanded formulation of the relationship between child care and child quality. More general notions of child care are considered to complete the discussion.

Noncustodial market-supplied day care can be incorporated into the analysis by augmenting the description of child quality technology; that is, a description of how day care affects child quality. Presumably, the effect of day care on child quality is directly related to the time spent in such care. Assume for the moment that day care is detrimental to child quality. Each additional hour supplied to the labor market exposes the child to another hour of day care which reduces child quality. Recall, with the use of neutral custodial day care, the net value of market work equals the net wage (market wage rate less day care costs). Now that day care reduces child quality, the net value of market work declines by the additional cost of reduced child quality. Hence, women will perform less market work than when day care's impact on child quality is neutral. Conversely, day care that is beneficial to child quality provides an additional incentive for market work. The net market wage is augmented by the value of the addition to child quality. Though the net value of market work changes by whether day care is detrimental, neutral or beneficial to child quality, the remaining structure of the economic framework is unchanged. However, permitting day care to directly influence the level of child quality provides another incentive, or disincentive, for the use of day care. When day care is custodial, factors influence the usage of day care only through their effect on labor supply. Now these factors will directly affect day care usage as a source of child quality. Hence, the previous discussion on the effect of various changes on child quality also applies to day care.

The preceding discussion recognizes that day care may affect child quality. The discussion assumes that a unit of child quality is the same regardless of whether it is produced in the household or purchased in the market via day care. Yet, it is also reasonable to assume that household and market-produced child care are *not* perfect substitutes. The care received in the market is in some sense different from the care received in the home. The easiest way to incorporate this notion is to recognize that child care is a multidimensional, not a one dimensional service. Thus, instead of mapping child care into a one dimensional commodity called child quality, Q, the analysis must admit a multidimensional child care vector, Q_1, Q_2, . . . Q_k.[11] Child care in the home may offer one bundle of services while day care may offer another bundle. By this perspective, child care is not the same service unless all of the components of the bundle are equal. The description of household preferences must also be expanded. In the expanded model, household preferences are defined over the composite commodity, Z, and the characteristics of child care, Q_1 . . . Q_k. Similarly, instead of a single household technology for the production of Q, the household possesses a technology for each of the care dimensions. Although this is more complicated because of the additional dimensions of child care, the household solves its consumption and resource allocation decision according to the same two-step process that was described previously.

Some of the additional dimensions of child care deserve mention. First, the multidimensional aspect of child care implies that tradeoffs exist between care dimensions. Parents may be willing to accept reduced learning opportunities for a healthier and safer environment. Moreover, households value characteristics differently, so that otherwise similar households may consume different types of care.[12]

Second, the multidimensional aspect of child care quality provides a rationale for the diversity in the types of child-care providers—different dimensions of care may be best supplied by different types of providers. In this framework, in-home maternal child care is one type, in-home nonrelative care may be another, as is the care provided in a family home or in a center. While each mode of child care may offer some amounts of each characteristic of care, different modes may produce different characteristics most cheaply. Hence, for fixed levels of the characteristics, "best" means "least cost." For example, cognitive skills may be produced most efficiently by the mother at home while it may be cheapest to develop the child's social skills in center-based care. The household will combine both types of care to obtain the desired level of characteristics. Consequently, households may use different modes of care because their relative valuation of characteristics differ or because of cost differences across suppliers. An increase of household income induces change in the intensive margin (increased consumption of characteristics already selected) and in the extensive margin (commence consuming characteristics not already selected). Substitution effects across different characteristics and modes exist for changes in the relative prices of care.

3.0 *Empirical Evidence of Changing Incentives for Day Care Usage*

The economic framework is used in this section to organize the discussion of the empirical evidence on the changing incentives for day-care use. The discussion considers first factors which are connected directly with the increase in female labor-force participation. The discussion then considers factors that have changed the choice of day-care mode.

The analysis begins with evidence on the secular pattern of female labor-force participation. Table 1 presents the number of children with mothers in the labor force for the period 1970-85. The top portion of the table reports the total number of children under age six, the percentage of children with working mothers and the total number with working mothers. The same information for infants (children under the age of 1) is reported in the bottom portion of the table. The absolute number of preschool children with working mothers has increased dramatically during this fifteen-year period. For children under the age of six, the percent increase between 1970 and 1985 is 74 percent, while for infants the number increased a remarkable 84 percent during the ten year period 1975 to 1985. Moreover, the growth in the absolute number of children with working mothers is due almost entirely to an increase in the labor-force participation rate of their mothers. The absolute number of children in the two age groups is approximately the same during the period 1970 to 1985, while the labor-force participation rates for the mothers of these children increased substantially. By 1985, nearly half of all children under the age of six had mothers in the labor force; even 48 percent of all infants in 1985 had working mothers.

To observe that more women are working is hardly novel; the increased labor-force participation by women has been well documented and is an intensively studied phenomenon. As suggested by Table 1, what has changed in recent years is the increased labor- force participation by mothers, especially mothers with young children. To highlight these trends, Table 2 reports female labor-force participation rates separately by age, marital status and age of the youngest child for wives (husband present). The purpose of the three panels of Table 2 is to place the labor-force participation rates of women living in traditional families (married) and assuming traditional roles (with children) in relation to patterns associated with the larger population of women. Each panel of Table 2 reports labor-force participation rates for a more narrowly defined group of women, culminating with the group assuming a traditional role, "married with children." Panel A reports age-specific female labor-force participation rates for women under age 65. From panel A, the predominate increase in female labor-force participation has occurred among the three youngest age groups reporᴛed. These age groups span the primary childbearing years. In panel B, labor-force participation rates for the period 1970-1985 are reported by age and by marital status. These participation rates increased for all but the youngest age group of single women reported in Panel B. Married women have the lowest participation rates of all marital statuses. For all age groups, married women have experienced the largest percentage increase in their participation rates. Panel C reports the labor-force participation rates of married women by the age of their youngest child for the period 1970-1985. The labor-force behavioral patterns reported in Panel C mimic those reported in Table 1.[13] Using slightly different age groupings for the children, the substantial rise in labor-force activity of married women matches quite well the increase for all women reported in Table 1. Most striking is the near doubling (25.8 percent to 50.7 percent) of the proportion of working wives with young children (less than age 3) over this fifteen-year period.

The behavior reported in Tables 1 and 2 of the increased attachment by women, especially women with children, to the labor market reflects a new reality of the woman's role in today's society. The secular growth in labor-force activity by women with young children provides a clear explanation as to why day care has entered public debate.

Labor-force participation statistics do not measure the type of jobs held by women. Increased labor-force participation will affect the demand for day care depending on the types of jobs employing women. To assess the impact on the demand for day care, it is important to consider the average hours worked by women and the occupational structure of their jobs. Table 3 reports the distribution of hours worked by women during the period 1960-1980. Through 1980, the distribution of hours of work shows little movement toward part-time work schedules. Long full-time work weeks (more than 40 hours per week) are less common in 1980 than in 1960, but a substantial shift toward part-time work (less than 35 hours per week) is not present. Furthermore, occupational distributions by gender show little movement away from women holding "traditional female jobs" (Killingsworth and Heckman (1986) or Bergmann (1989)). While the workplace in the future may be more receptive to "flex-schedule" and "work sharing," ideas that make child care easier to arrange within the household, the current situation is best characterized as a continuation of historical trends.

Tables 1 through 3 and the accompanying discussion relate to the extensive margin of nonmaternal child care; as more women work, the joint nature of market participation and nonmaternal child care implies that the usage of day care will increase. Thus factors that increase female participation also produce a general increase in the use of day care.[14] These statistics do not provide insight into the changes affecting the choice of child-care mode used. Table 4 reports usage statistics on the type of preschool child care selected by working mothers during the period 1965-85. In Table 4, relative care includes care by the child's father, sibling, grandparent, or other family relative (Hofferth (1988) p. 6). The other categories in the table

are self-explanatory. The first two forms of care are frequently provided in the child's home, while the latter two modes are provided
outside the child's home.

The shift in the location of the care is dramatic. Assuming that all
the relative care is provided in the child's home, in 1965 approximately three quarters (77 percent) of all care was provided in the
child's home; by 1985 only approximately half of all preschool children received care in their home (54 percent). Even including the
father, relative care declined steadily, falling 14 percentage points (22
percent) over the period. This decline is matched by a substantial
increase in the use of center-based care (17 percentage points).
Although less striking, use of family home care increased slightly
over this period. Not only are there more children with working
mothers (Tables 1 and 2), working about the same hours (Table 3), but
also an increased proportion of the children are cared for outside of
the family's home (Table 4).

The economic framework of the previous section can be applied to
understand this changing pattern of child-care usage. Increased participation of women in the labor market has two effects on day-care
usage. First, as discussed above, the joint nature of labor-force participation and day care implies that increased market activity by
women increases the use of day care. Second and more subtle, the
increased labor-market participation by women of all ages reduces
the supply of in-home child-care providers. The observed decline in
relative care is consistent with the increased female labor force participation rates of Table 2. Increased attachment to the labor market
also reduces the number of unpaid providers. By the reduced availability of providers, women must resort to market care (family home
and center care). In terms of the economic model of Section 2, the
reduced supply of informal providers increases the price of relative
care, causing households to substitute away from that form of care.

The reduction in relative care is also consistent with other aspects
of the changing household structure. As is well known, the twentieth
century has witnessed increased urbanization and the decline of the
extended family. Parents are less likely to live with their adult children and the mobility of modern society means that the distance
between family members has increased. These factors operate independently of the increase in the female participation rate to reduce
the available supply of relative providers.

A second change in household structure is the recent increase in
divorce rates. Stable until the mid-1960's, divorce rates doubled over

the span of ten years and have remained constant since.[15] Moreover, women are more likely to head families. This rise in female headship is documented in Table 5. For whites and blacks the proportion of female-headed households has increased since 1970. The proportion of families headed by a woman is higher for blacks than for whites. Since 1970, however, the growth rate of the number of female-headed families for both racial groups has been substantial, 53 percent for blacks and 41 percent for whites. There are important differences across racial groups. For whites, the proportion single (never-married) has been a modest yet growing fraction of the households. For blacks, the share of never-married females has more than doubled during the same period (16.2 percent to 33.4 percent). For whites, divorce has surpassed widowhood as the primary cause of headship. One impact of the marital instability on children is shown in the bottom portion of Table 5. The proportion of female-headed households containing at least one child increased for whites and remained approximately constant for blacks. The average number of children in these households declined, substantially for blacks, minimally for whites. White female-headed households are more likely to contain a child; they also contain fewer children in 1985 than in 1970. During the same period, the average number of children per black female-headed family is lower, reflecting the reduction in average family size that occurred during this period.

A direct effect of the increased marital instability is that women are less likely to have a spouse present to help provide care. In terms of the economic model of section 2, increased marital instability reduces the time endowment of the woman's household. Also, upon divorce women experience a substantial decline in their income (Garfinkel, 1987). The severe loss of resources requires many of these women to enter the labor market in order to support their families. Usage of market-supplied child care increases in response to the reductions of household resources.

There are indirect effects of the higher divorce rates on labor-supply behavior of women (and hence on child-care choice) that are not easily incorporated into the (one-period) economic model of section 2 but which deserve mention.[16] If women anticipate that marriages are more likely to end, their (expected) wealth within marriage declines.[17] The reduction in (expected) wealth increases the labor-force participation of women (Johnson and Skinner 1986). Also, if market skills depreciate with disuse (Mincer and Polachek 1974), married women facing a greater risk of divorce have an incentive to maintain their attachment to the market.

Reduced availability of relative care reduces the household's time and income endowments; equivalently, the shadow price of relative care has increased. Has the cost of relative care increased to the household? Information is scarce, but the figures reported in Table 6 from Hofferth (1988) suggest that the answer is yes.[18] The constant dollar hourly expenditure of all modes of child care increased from the mid-70's to mid- 80's. The cost of relative care increased 58 percent, while that of family day care increased 7 percent and center care 15 percent. Most importantly, the reported hourly payment between relative care and other arrangements moved against relative care: day care in a family home was 52 percent more expensive than relative care in 1975, but only 4 percent more expensive in 1985. This change in the relative prices of the method of child care provides another rationale for the shift to out-of-home providers and away from relative and in-home providers.

Changes in government policies and programs affect the incentives for the use of day care. Two changes in government policies and programs have a direct effect on these trends. First, as previously discussed, a tax credit for child-care expenditures was legislated in 1976. This tax expenditure program is the largest federal policy supporting child care (Robins 1988). Record-keeping requirements to document child-care expenditures favor the use of larger, more formal providers of day care such as center-based group care. This facet of the program reduces the relative price of the more formal providers of day care. The tax credit subsidizes paid market care (Hotz 1988). Nonrefundability of the tax credit limits its value to many low-income families. Families on AFDC and other low-income families are more likely to use relative-provided care or other forms of care which are unpaid or paid in-kind than are higher-income groups (Brush 1987). Both of these mechanisms create distributional effects which favor middle- and upper-income families.

The second government policy change was the general trend toward decentralization and deregulation during the Reagan years (Kahn and Kammerman 1988). The Omnibus Budget Reconciliation Act of 1981 eliminated much of the direct federal funding for child care services. Although cuts to the Head Start Program were later restored, in constant dollars, direct federal support for the provision of child care has declined since the mid-1970's (Robins 1988). Federal regulation of the day-care industry also lessened as proposed national quality standards and licensing requirements were cancelled in 1981. Local governments regulate day-care providers, consequently rules and regulations vary substantially across regions. Nearly all of the family home providers (90-94 percent) are unlicensed (Hofferth and Phillips 1987). Since a substantial portion of suppliers never appear on official rolls, direct evidence on the type and quality of care received in the market is almost completely lacking.[19] Unconstrained by evidence, each side in the public debate may freely speculate on the consequences of the absence of federal standards. Some argue that costs of center and family home care have remained low because of the absence of regulation. Minimal regulation also keeps entry barriers low so that new providers can easily enter to meet the increased demand. Competitive pressure from a large potential supply works to keep prices low. Others argue that the quality of care is too low or has fallen in the absence of federal legislation. The lack of minimum care standards means that some children could be exposed to unsafe and harmful care. Even if the private cost of unsafe and harmful care is low, the social cost of such care is not. It is interesting to note that major recent child care bills before Congress have included the establishment of minimum quality standards (Stephen *et al.*, 1988 and Institute for Research on Poverty, 1989). This new legislation will have a direct influence on the cost and quality of care available in the market.

No discussion of changing incentives for day care use would be complete without recognizing that a potentially large factor may be changing preferences and willingness of households to use day care. Many economists use household production models to avoid attributing changing consumption patterns to changes in "tastes."[20] Yet that possibility cannot be dismissed. As more households use day care, it becomes socially more acceptable for others to use it as well; there is less social stigma attached to using day care. Household perceptions on the impact of day care on child development also appear to be changing. The view that day care is always detrimental to the child's health and development has been softened by recent research. Kahn and Kammerman (1987, p. 15) note that:

> There is no credible evidence that good child care programs are harmful to children's parental attachments, intellectual development, or general growth. Good programs are those that have small groups, high proportions of staff to children and well-trained caregivers.

The effect of day care on child development and growth is far from settled. As information and experience accumulates on the effect of day care on children, we should be better able to design healthy, safe, and enriching environments for children away from home. If this assessment is true, then parental willingness to use day care will continue to increase. If the opposite turns out to be true, we can expect that the use of day care will diminish, implying that more parental time will be used instead. The impact on day-care usage from this potential shift in preferences could be substantial and could dominate the other (economic) factors discussed above.

4.0 Incentives for Corporations to Use Day Care

The previous sections have examined the changing incentives facing individuals for the use of day care. This section examines the incentives facing corporations. The primary thesis of this discussion is that corporates face few incentives to increase involvement in the provision of day care.

The increased demand for out-of-home care generated by the recent increase in female labor force participation coupled with large cutbacks in direct federal subsidies for publicly supplied day care have led many to turn to the corporations to become active in the supply of day care. To date, such requests have stimulated little interest on the part of corporations. Kahn and Kammerman (1987, p. 175) note that by 1986, 2,000-3,000 employers *nationwide* sponsored some form of child-care services. The form of this sponsorship varied greatly, with the bulk of the corporate effort assuming the form of flexible benefit and salary-reduction plans, referral services, or the arrangement of modest employee discounts available at local suppliers. Direct corporate involvement in the provision of day care for its employees has been limited almost exclusively to hospitals.

The lack of direct corporate involvement reflects the limited incentives for corporations to offer this care. To offer day care to its employees requires that the corporation enter a new line of business. The required expertise is unfamiliar to many firms; it is not surprising that hospitals and members of the health-care industry account for the large majority of on-site employer care. Additional barriers are present. On-site care exposes the corporation to the same licensing requirements and legal liability in case of accidents as any other provider of group care. Among the benefits accruing to corporate suppliers of on-site day care are reduced employee absenteeism and turnover and increased employee productivity. The evidence on the extent of these benefits is mixed.[21]

Corporations do not have to become involved in the direct provision of child care to help increase the supply of child-care services.

There are two types of fringe benefits that help parents with child care. "Flexible benefit plans" offer employees a fixed-dollar value of benefits which can be allocated in any fashion to the menu of programs offered by the corporation. Child-care services are one of the choices on the benefit menu. Flexible-spending accounts are the second type of fringe benefit. These are salary-reduction programs whereby the employer maintains an account for the employee and pays out funds for specific expenditures.[22] Funds allocated to the accounts are not subject to federal income tax or FICA (Federal Insurance Contributions Act, e.g., social security and medicare taxes). A maximum of $5,000 may be allocated for dependent care assistance. Any funds remaining in the account at year end are forfeited by the employee. Child-care expenses in excess of $5,000 are eligible for child-care tax credit. These funds offer employees the equivalent of a dependent child tax deduction. A small incentive is provided to the employer to establish these accounts, as the corporation does not pay FICA on employee salary allocated to the fund. Morris (1987, p. 2) notes that these plans offer no "special tax incentives that make it more attractive for employers to spend money on day care for its employees than to provide some other kind of fringe benefit."

Employers have been unwilling to extend these types of fringe-benefit programs because such programs appeal to a small clientele within the firm. Unlike major medical, dental, and eye-care programs, which are usable by all employees, day-care programs would be used by a fraction of all employees and even then, only for a limited number of years. Indeed, as Robins (1988) shows, parents represent a smaller portion of the workforce in 1985 than they did in 1968.

Corporate incentives for offering child-care benefits appear to be small to nonexistent. Employers wish to avoid the development of costly benefits that appeal to a relatively small number of workers. Employees wish to maintain a separation of their work environment and the quality of child care. Fringe benefits and other nonwage sources of compensation frequently are seen as a means to attract labor. The sizeable inflow of women and especially women with children witnessed during the last fifteen years suggest that these benefits are *not* required to induce women into the market.

5.0 *Conclusion*

This paper has presented a framework for understanding the changing incentives for the usage of day care. While there have been few changes for corporations, during the last twenty years the incentives facing individuals have changed. Changes in household composition, and structure, marital stability, government policies, consumer perceptions of the effects of day care on child development and factors inducing women into the labor market are contributing factors to the increased use of day care. While assessment of causality is impossible with the available data, the fact that women have responded to these incentives is clear: by 1985, over 50 percent of the women with children under the age of three worked in the market. Trends in female labor-force participation suggest that this increased involvement in the labor market by women is unlikely to abate. Women with preschool children will continue to work and will require day care for their young children. Future research must address how best to provide that care.

—James R. Walker is assistant professor of economics at the University of Wisconsin—Madison.

All opinions are those of the author and not necessarily the views of The Rockford Institute or The University of Wisconsin. I thank Glen Cain, Charles Manski, J. Karl Scholz and participants of the Labor Workshop at the University of Wisconsin-Madison for helpful comments.

ENDNOTES

[1] Clearly, men also provide child care and produce child quality. This assumption is made for expositional purposes.

[2] The fixed-proportion technology is used for expositional purposes.

[3] A restrictive feature of this technology is that it does not permit substitution between time and goods inputs to produce a fixed level of output. In general, a variety of input combinations could be used to produce any level of output. The household (or firm) selects the optimal combination of inputs. The assumption of a fixed-proportion technology eliminates this choice.

[4] The simple linear function for the price of child quality is specific to the fixed-proportion technology.

[5] Remember, to keep the exposition simple, I have considered household production to be confined to one activity, the production of child quality. Certainly, many household activities can be classified as household production (Becker 1965).

[6] See Willis (1974) for a similar prediction on the income effect on the demand for children by working and nonworking women.

[7] Knowledge, sometimes called human capital, is an integral part of technology. Human capital is accumulated via education, training and experience. By the dissemination of new ideas and techniques, education plays a central role in the adoption of new techniques and procedures and hence on technological change. Education enhances market skills and may enhance nonmarket or household production skills. Thus technological change encompasses more than simply "machines."

[8]Some will argue that scale effects dominate the labor-saving impacts of innovation: improved household technology also leads to larger houses, more clothes, more dishes, etc.

[9]The optimal input ratio of time to goods is α/β. A decline in α means that less time is required to produce the prechange output. Denote this released time as δt. Sold to the market, this released time earns $W\delta t$ which can be used to buy additional market goods.

[10]Lewis and Morrison (1988) calculate budget sets that incorporate dependencies among several social programs and taxes.

[11]An analogy to automobiles may be useful. A Ford and a Rolls-Royce are both automobiles yet are viewed as different products because they differ in their underlying characteristics e.g., comfort and smoothness of ride, handling, gasoline mileage, acceleration, prestige. Child-care arrangements that differ in convenience (Q_1), reliability (Q_2), safety (Q_3), flexibility (Q_4), learning (Q_5) or nurturing (Q_6) are different services.

[12]In the restricted model of the previous section, differences in preferences across households translate into different willingness to exchange Q for Z. For example, households may vary in the relative value attached to child quality.

[13]One difference is that the labor-force participation rates in Table 1 are for all women, those reported in Panel C are for married women.

[14]The rise in female labor-force participation has been extensively studied by social scientists from all disciplines. To evaluate the causal mechanisms generating the increased female labor-force participation is beyond the scope of the paper. In fact, a convincing analysis of this phenomenon still awaits. Smith and Ward (1989) provide a recent, if controversial, analysis on the mechanisms drawing women into the labor market. Other studies on this important issue include the special volume of *The Journal of Labor Economics* (1985) edited by Layard and Mincer; the symposium on Women in the Labor Market, edited by Lazear appearing in *The Journal of Economic Perspectives* (1989); Killingsworth and Heckman (1986); and Gunderson (1989).

[15]The number of divorces per 1,000 married women age 15 and older was 8.8 in 1940, 10.3 in 1950, 9.2 in 1960, 10.6 in 1965, 20.3 in 1975 and 21.5 in 1985 (*Statistical Abstract of the United States*, various issues).

[16]These effects illustrate that life-cycle considerations create additional paths and mechanisms that affect household decision-making. A more complete model of household decision-making would extend the model of section 2 to include these life-cycle aspects.

[17]An increased divorce probability reduces the likelihood that a husband's income will be available. Hence the (expected) resources of the household declines.

[18]These statistics are from self-reported consumer surveys on child-care expenditures. As such they do not control for the quality of the care received or for possible compositional effects of the samples. Strictly speaking, these data are not prices.

[19]See, however, Kisker *et al.* (1989) for a discussion of a promising (if geographically limited) new survey and study.

[20]However, see the lucid discussion on this point in Deaton and Muellbauer (1980), pp. 245-250.

[21]See, O'Connell and Bloom (1987) and Kahn and Kammerman (1987) p. 179.

[22]The following statement of the tax law draws on Morris (1987).

References

Becker, Gary S. (1960), "An Economic Analysis of Fertility," in *Demographic and Economic Change in Developed Countries*, Universities-National Bureau Conference Series, No. 11, Princeton, NJ: Princeton University Press.

Becker, Gary S. (1965), "A Theory of the Allocation of Time," *Economic Journal* 75: 493-517.

Bergmann, Barbara R. (1989), "Does the Market for Women's Labor Need Fixing?" *Journal of Economic Perspectives* 3 (Winter): 43-60.

Brush, Lorelei (1987), "Child Care Used by Working Women in the AFDC Population: An Analysis of the SIPP Data Base," Unpublished Manuscript.

Deaton, Angus and J. Muellbauer (1980), *Economics and Consumer Behavior*, New York: Cambridge University Press.

Garfinkel, Irvin (1987), "Welfare Policy in America," Discussion Paper 847-87, Institute for Research on Poverty, University of Wisconsin-Madison.

Gunderson, Morley (1989), "Male-Female Wage Differentials and Policy Responses," *Journal of Economic Literature* 27 (March): 46-72.

Hayghe, Howard (1986), "Rise in Mothers' Labor Force Activity Includes Those with Infants," *Monthly Labor Review* (February): 43-45.

Heckman, James J. (1974), "Effects of Child Care Programs on Women's Work Effort," in *Economics of the Family*, edited by T.W. Schultz, Chicago, IL: University of Chicago Press.

Hofferth, Sandra (1988), "The Current Child Care Debate in Context," Unpublished Manuscript, April 1988.

Hofferth, Sandra and D. Phillips (1987), "Child Care in the United States, 1970-1995," *Journal of Marriage and the Family* 49 (August): 559-571.

Hotz, V. Joseph (1988), "The Effects of Child Care Costs and Policies of Female Labor Force Participation: What Do We Know?" Unpublished Manuscript, University of Chicago.

Institute for Research on Poverty (1989), "The Family Support Act of 1988," *Focus*, University of Wisconsin- Madison, Winter 1988-89.

Johnson, William and J. Skinner (1986), "Labor Supply and Marital Separation," *American Economic Review* 76 (September): 455-469.

Kahn, Alfred and S. Kammerman (1987), *Child Care: Facing the Hard Choices*, Dover, MA: Auburn House Press.

Killingsworth, Mark R. (1983), *Labor Supply*, New York: Cambridge University Press.

Killingsworth, Mark R. and J. Heckman (1986), "Female Labor Supply: A Survey," in *Handbook of Labor Economics*, Vol. 1, edited by O.C. Ashenfelter and R. Layard, Amsterdam: North- Holland Publishing Company.

Kisker, Ellen, R. Maynard, A. Gordon and M. Strain (1989), "The Child Care Challenge: What Parents Need and What Is Available in Three Metropolitan Areas," Unpublished paper, Mathematics Policy Research, Princeton, NJ.

Layard, Richard and J. Mincer (eds) (1985), "Trends in Women's Work, Education, and Family Building," *Journal of Labor Economics* 3 (January, Supplement).

Lazear, Edward P. (1989), "Symposium on Women in the Labor Market," *The Journal of Economic Perspectives* 3 (Winter): 3-9.

Lewis, G.H., and R.J. Morrison (1988), "Interactions Among Social Welfare Programs," Discussion Paper 866-88, Institute for Research on Poverty, University of Wisconsin-Madison.

Mincer, Jacob and S. Polacheck (1974), "Family Investments in Human Capital: Earnings of Women," in *Economics of the Family*, edited by T.W. Schultz, Chicago, IL: University of Chicago Press.

Morris, Marie B. (1987), "Day Care Services: Current Tax Laws," Paper 87-680A, Congressional Research Service, Library of Congress, July 15, 1987.

O'Connell, Martin and D. Bloom (1987), "Juggling Jobs and Babies: America's Child Care Challenge," Publication No. 12, Population Reference Bureau.

Robins, Phillip K. (1988), "Federal Financing of Child Care: Alternative Approaches and Economic Implications," Unpublished paper, University of Miami, Miami, Florida.

Smith, James P. and M. Ward (1989), "Women in the Labor Market and in the Family," *Journal of Economic Perspectives* 3 (Winter): 9-24.

Stephan, Sharon, A. Stewart and M. Morris (1988), "Child Day Care: Summaries of Selected Major Bills in the 100th Congress," Paper 88-321EPW, Congressional Research Service, Library of Congress, May 17, 1988.

U.S. Department of Commerce, Bureau of Census (1988), *Statistical Abstract of the United States*, Washington, D.C.: U.S. Government Printing Office.

Willis, Robert J. (1974), "Economic Theory of Fertility Behavior," in *Economics of the Family*, edited by T.W. Schultz, Chicago, IL: University of Chicago Press.

Table 1
Actual Number of Children with Mothers in the Labor Force
All Races
(in Thousands)

Group	1970	1975	1980	1985
Total number of children	20,923	19,667	19,639	21,584
% with mothers in Labor Force	29	36	43	49
Number of children with mothers in labor force	6,068	7,080	8,445	10,576
Total number of children < age 1	3,508	3,512	3,561	3,742
% with mothers in Labor Force	n.a	31*	38	48
Number of children with mothers in labor force	—	977	1,353	1,796

Notes:
 *Based on data from 1976.
Source: Hofferth and Phillips (1987) Table 1.

Table 2
Labor Force Participation Rates of Women
Selected Years

Panel A: All Women, By Age

Year/Age	20-24	25-34	35-44	45-54	55-64
1970	57.7	45.0	51.1	54.4	43.0
1975	64.1	54.9	55.8	54.6	40.9
1980	68.9	65.5	65.5	59.9	41.3
1985	71.8	70.9	71.8	64.4	42.0

Panel B: By Marital Status and Age

	Single (Never Married)			Married (Husband Present)			Divorced, Widowed & Separated		
Year	20-24	25-34	35-44	20-24	25-34	35-44	20-24	25-34	35-44
1970	71.1	80.7	73.3	47.4	39.3	47.2	59.7	65.1	67.9
1975	69.5	80.4	77.8	57.3	48.3	51.9	68.1	67.5	69.5
1980	72.2	84.2	78.5	60.5	59.3	62.5	68.5	77.1	76.4
1985	64.9	82.5	80.6	64.9	65.6	68.1	66.5	78.9	80.6

Panel C: Wives, Husband Present By Age of Youngest Child

		No Children	With Children				
Year	All	age < 18	Total age < 18	age 3 or less	ages 3-5	ages 6-13	ages 14-17
1970	40.8	42.2	39.8	25.8	36.9	47.0	54.8
1975	44.5	44.0	44.9	32.8	42.2	51.8	53.8
1980	50.2	46.0	54.3	41.5	51.7	62.6	60.5
1985	54.3	48.3	61.3	50.7	58.6	68.1	67.0

Source: Panels A and B: The Statistical Abstract of the United States (1988)
Panel C: Hayghe (1986), Table 1.

Table 3
Distribution of Hours Worked of Employed Females During Census Week
From the Decennial Census of Population, By Year

Hours	1950	1960	1970	1980
1-34	20.6	27.7	31.5	30.8
35-40	52.9	54.3	56.4	56.4
≥ 41	26.6	18.1	11.7	12.8

Source: Adapted from Killingsworth and Heckman (1986), Table 2-10.

Table 4
Percentage of Preschool Children with Working Mothers in Each Type of Care, 1965-1985

Type of Care	1965	1977	1982	1985
Relative	62	58	55	48
Sitter	15	7	6	6
Family Day Care Home	18	23	23	22
Day Care Center	6	13	15	23

Source: Hofferth (1988), Reported in Figure 1.

Table 5
Female Family Householders with No Spouse Present, Characteristics by Race
1970 to 1986

	White			Black		
	1970	1980	1985	1970	1980	1985
Female Family Householders Percent of all Families	9.1	11.6	12.8	28.3	40.3	43.3
Median Age (years)	50.4	43.7	42.7	41.3	37.4	38.0
Marital Status:						
Single (never married)	9.2	10.6	11.9	16.2	27.3	33.4
Married (spouse absent)	18.5	16.9	16.0	39.7	28.6	21.1
Widowed	47.0	32.7	28.3	29.9	22.2	21.2
Divorced	25.3	39.8	43.8	14.2	21.9	24.5
Presence of Children						
No Own Children	52.0	41.2	43.5	33.5	28.1	34.5
With Own Children	48.0	58.8	56.5	66.6	71.9	65.5
Mean Number of Children	1.00	1.03	0.96	1.83	1.51	1.29

Source: Statistical Abstract of the United States (1988), Table 70.

Table 6
Mean Hourly Payment by Mothers Paying for Care
By Type of Arrangement and Survey Year

Year	Relative	Day Care Home	Center & Nursery School
1975	0.36	0.55	0.60
1976-77	—	—	0.65
1977-78	—	0.59	—
1985	1.14	1.17	1.37
Deflated to 1975 Dollars	0.57	0.59	0.69

Source: Hofferth (1988), Table 1.

The Economics of Day Care Legislation: A Public Choice Perspective

by Deborah Walker

Introduction

Child care is now considered one of the most important issues facing the American family. It is not, as if often cited, a "female issue." It is a parental issue, a problem faced by both mothers and fathers alike. It is an issue that two-income families, in which both the mother and father choose to work outside of the home, face. It is an issue faced by the growing number of single-parent households. And now, due to the drive for more extensive national day-care legislation, it is an issue that all taxpayers must consider.

Those who either demand or supply day care, and those who directly pay for it will certainly feel the effects of a national day-care policy. However, there are many individuals in our society who will be indirectly affected by such legislation. And furthermore, the individuals directly affected could find that the legislation leads to unintended consequences, consequences that are in direct opposition to the initial goal or purpose of the legislation.

The purpose of this paper is to analyze proposed day-care legislation using what can be considered a "public choice" perspective. The methodology of most economists working in the area of public choice is individualistic. That is, it "begins with the acting or decision-making individual," particularly as that individual "participates in the processes through which group choices are organized."[1] As James Buchanan and Gordon Tullock do in *The Calculus of Consent*, I assume that individuals are different and that they will therefore have different goals in mind for the outcome of collective action.[2] I assume that in most cases, people act in their own self-interest. However, this "interest" can take many forms, monetary and non-monetary alike. Furthermore, as stated earlier, people may not be aware of the outcomes of what they propose. Insofar as they are incorrect in assessing these outcomes, they are not acting in their own self-interest, but believe they are.[3]

Therefore, the analysis that follows is an attempt to recognize those individuals in our society who would experience a net benefit from day-care legislation and those individuals who would experience, on net, a cost. As public-choice theory also tells us, those who feel they would benefit from this legislation will be those most vocal in trying to get the legislation passed. This is true as long as the cost of lobbying is lower than the perceived benefit of getting the legislation passed (taking into consideration the uncertainty that the lobbying may not be effective). The costs of organizing lobbying efforts will depend upon the number of individuals involved, how closely they all agree upon the issue, and geographic dispersion. Some individuals who may perceive a benefit may not actually lobby for the legislation because of the costs involved.[4]

The Proposed Legislation

There are two basic forms of legislation now proposed. The Act for Better Childcare Services of 1989 (S. 1885)[5], or the "ABC" Bill, calls for extensive federal grants for the expansion and regulation of day care facilities. On the other hand, a variety of tax-credit plans have also been introduced. President Bush, for example, has proposed a family tax-credit plan which would give a family a $1,000 tax cut per child under age four to families earning less than $20,000 annually.[6]

The ABC Bill

The ABC Bill is more complicated than a tax-credit system and would lead to different economic outcomes. Furthermore, there are a larger number of individuals involved in this bill, making the analysis much more extensive. A summary of the basic recommendations of the bill is necessary before actually analyzing the many individuals most likely to be affected by its passage.

One main purpose of the ABC Bill is to increase the supply of existing day-care facilities, especially to low-income families. In order to achieve this goal, section 8 of the bill provides for direct assistance to parents through child-care "certificates" which can be used to buy child care from eligible child-care providers; grants to the eligible child-care providers themselves; and grants to government units that agree to contract with eligible child-care providers. The vast majority of the funds allocated for this legislation would be used for this purpose.

However, the bill also calls for funding of the following: minimum national quality standards control, enforcement of licensing and regulatory requirements, training and technical assistance for child-care providers, resource and referral programs, increased salaries and scholarships for child-care providers, and data-collection services to determine the necessary information for all of the above.

It is important to note that state-licensed or regulated private day-care providers would be eligible for the funds. However, if they accept them, they must comply with the regulatory standards as dictated by the federal legislation. State standards would not be lowered to meet federal standards. The stricter standards would always apply. Church-based day-care centers are also eligible. However, section 20 of the bill states that those centers that do receive funds cannot discriminate on the basis of religion.

The Beneficiaries

There have been many different individuals lobbying in favor of the ABC Bill. The most obvious are state officials, particularly governors of those states which would receive the largest percentages of the federal funds provided by the bill.[7]

The allotment to each state would depend upon the number of children in the state who are less than 5 years of age as compared to the same number nationally, the number of children receiving free or reduced-price lunches in the state as compared to the same figure nationally, and the per capita income of the state as compared to the same figure nationally.

The reason that state and local officials may be very interested in passing the legislation is not always to "help working parents." But instead, to increase the possibility of re-election by pleasing as many constituents as possible.

Since a state or local politician transfers wealth for the benefit of special-interest groups and himself at the expense of others (the taxpayer and other special-interest groups), he tries to minimize any conflicts of interest that may arise among his constituents.

With regard to the ABC Bill, the greatest lobbying efforts will be by those state and local officials who have the largest number of constituents who have children under the age of five. Also the officials in states with an average income level less than the national average will also have a large incentive to support the bill.

However, the problem with using the criteria ascribed by the ABC Bill for allocating funds specifically for lower-income child-care purposes is that in any given locale those with children under the age of five may not be those with income levels less than the national average. A state may receive a greater proportion of funds because it has both a high percentage of people with young children and a high percentage of people with income levels less than the national average.

Insofar as this is the case, high-income families in some states would be subsidized by taxpayers nationally. Furthermore, even if the majority of families with young children in a state are low-income families, they may not use institutionalized day care as extensively as do higher-income families.

On the other side of the lobbying effort will be those officials in states that primarily consist of the following demographics: families without children, single individuals, and retired individuals. More federal funds (through taxation) will flow out of these states than will flow in in accordance with the ABC Bill.

Other individuals and/or institutions in favor of the ABC Bill include Head Start agencies, public agencies that provide social services or human resources, heads of local education agencies, and heads of resource, information, and referral agencies. The reason behind their support of the ABC Bill is clear. The bill would increase the demand for their services and/or increase the size of their budgets. As William Niskanan proposes, bureaucratic agencies produce the output level which will yield the highest possible budget because a bureaucrat's utility depends upon the size of his or her total budget (the use of which can then go to a number of things including salary, perks, regulation, power, etc.). This is true because bureaucrats do not have property rights to any amount which might be left over at the end of a budget period; therefore, this amount can only be claimed indirectly through budget expansion.[8]

This means that once the money has been budgeted to a bureau, there is no guarantee that the money will be used for the purpose that it was given. If a bureau is not able to (or purposefully does not) use the funds for the stated purpose by the end of the budget period, it will "expand" in other ways, such as obtain larger staffs and/or larger offices, for example. Any proposed bill which may call for the services of a particular bureau will have active testimony in its favor.

Among those that testified in favor of the ABC Bill are Richard M. Clifford, Associate Director of the Bush Institute for Child and Family Policy, and Lawrence J. Schweinhart of the High/Scope Educational Research Foundation. At first glance, it may appear that these research institutions are only testifying to give their "expert" opinions on what children need for a healthy development.

However, it is also true that the government would provide day-care services precisely because it is thought that the market alone is not doing an adequate job, either in terms of quantity or quality. Since those acting in the marketplace are not providing what parents "should" be demanding, we need research agencies filled with experts to tell parents, and the government-supported agencies, what they should be doing. Although the market is also influenced by "expert opinion," the final "experts" in the market are always the consumers. A private firm will only institute a policy recommended by a research institution if its consumers demand it to do so. There-fore, the research institution has to "sell" its ideas to consumers before they are accepted in the market.

This is not the case with government-operated or regulated firms. Research institutes can sell their ideas directly to the firms (usually at a much lower cost). Furthermore, these public firms are much more likely to accept the ideas because their knowledge of what to provide does not come from the competitive forces of the market. Since con-sumers are either forced to buy from one firm (in the case of a government-granted monopoly) or are faced with a fewer number of firms to choose among (in the case of government-subsidized or regu-lated market, i.e., the market for education), they cannot reveal their preferences to these firms as adequately as they can in a competitive market. Therefore, these firms must rely upon the opinion of experts (which are thought to be superior to the opinions of consumers—which, in many cases, is why the firm is government-operated or regulated in the first place).

The testimony of Lawrence J. Schweinhart of High/Scope Educa-tional Research Foundation reads: "Our mission is to develop, test, and disseminate applied knowledge of human development to the care and education of young people. . . . I encourage you to pass legislation that supports and assures the quality of early childhood programs. . . ."[9] This testimony is understandable in that the demand for institutionalized research centers such as his would most likely increase with a national day-care policy such as the one the ABC Bill proposes.[10]

Also testifying in favor of the ABC Bill are insurance companies. The understanding of their pro-ABC position becomes clear when viewed in light of the fact that insurance companies face the "moral hazard" problem and therefore it sometimes pays to police their cli-ents' behavior. If the government will do some or all of this policing for them through quality-control measures, their costs will decrease.

But also important are the contract terms between the insurance company and their clients. If the government states very specific guidelines which must be followed by a day-care center and an insurance contract includes a clause which states that the insurance company is not liable unless all federal or state specified guidelines are adhered to, the chances that an insurance company will be liable are decreased. The stricter the guidelines, the less responsible are the insurance companies.

Note the testimony of Arthur R. Nielsen, Senior Vice President of Underwriting in the Property and Casualty Group of CIGNA Corporation: "Mr. Chairman, there is no question that requiring adequate standards for child care is a key issue in providing insurance for child care centers . . . it has been our experience that the establishment of and adherence to sound, understandable, and *enforceable* risk selection standards and safety features are essential elements that enable us to offer adequate insurance coverage at fair and reasonable prices to day care centers throughout the country."[11]

As stated in the introduction of this paper, there are some individuals who may promote legislation that may not be in their self-interest, but who, because of their ignorance of the situation, support the legislation. Many parents may fall into this category.

The unintended consequences (unintended by some) of day-care regulation is to decrease the supply of the service. This is basic economics. Increase the cost of supplying something and the amount supplied will most likely decrease.

But what may be an even more important consequence of day care regulation is that it displaces the market quality-control mechanism. The "appropriate" quality of any service on the market will emerge over time as consumers respond to changes in the quality (and the sometimes-accompanying price changes) offered on the market.

This quality is controlled (or, in other words, contracts are upheld as promised) by several mechanisms on the market. The most obvious is the repeat-purchase mechanism. If a firm does not give the customer what he or she expected in terms of quality, the customer will not return and the value of the brand name or "reputation" of the firm will decline.[12] Other mechanisms noted by economists are price premiums (a higher price will mean a greater loss in terms of the future stream of income foregone if a firm cheats) and investment in firm-specific assets, such as logos and signs (which are nonsalvageable because the value of which go to zero if the firm cheats).[13] Furthermore, the fact that a firm simply advertises can guarantee quality because the more a firm advertises, the more its name is remembered. A firm will not want to be remembered as a "cheater."[14]

If government-mandated regulations are very different (or exceed) those that arise spontaneously on the market, it will be less profitable for private firms to enter the regulated industry. The usual market mechanisms used to control quality are replaced by government officials. The obvious incentive problem then arises. Not only do government officials have less interest in children than do the parents of children, but they also have less interest than do private firms in making sure the quality that parents want is provided as promised, the reason being the simple fact that if quality does decrease, the cost is not borne by the officials, as it would be borne by private firms in a non-regulated industry.

What happens, therefore, due to the regulations, is that day-care providers are driven underground so that they can avoid the regulations and/or licensing requirements. There will be no market advertising and very few of the other usual market mechanisms that arise to control quality. Therefore, parents must rely on word-of-mouth advertising, the word and experiences of friends and neighbors. What happens is that quality drastically declines.

Witness the testimony of Mrs. Linda Hartshorn. Mrs. Hartshorn's child, Danny, was beaten to death by his babysitter. Mrs. Hartshorn testified:

> Why did I choose this woman? She was a friend of ours; she asked to babysit for me. She was from a well-thought-of family, and my child was the only child she babysat for. From all outside appearances things appeared clean and safe— *perfect*.[15]

And consider the testimony of Cheri Robertson, another parent whose child was injured in a day care facility:

> As mothers we have to work, ultimately the responsibility of choosing day care is ours. We will accept that responsibility if you will guarantee us minimal standards.[16]

This statement tells us two things. This mother wants the state to take the responsibility of policing the quality of child care away from her. As government grows, individual responsibility gives way to "social responsibility."[17] Unfortunately, what this mother doesn't seem to understand is that "society" simply does not have the knowledge necessary to make her choices for her or the incentive to make the same choices she would make.

Parents who are supporting the ABC Bill because they feel it will increase the quality of child care providers may be making an error in judgment. Furthermore, parents who are supporting the ABC Bill because they think the overall cost (to them) of child care will decrease may also be making an error in judgment. The bill must be financed through taxation of one form or another.[18] It is always very difficult to determine the actual monetary cost (let alone costs in economic growth) of government-provided or subsidized services. The revenues alloted for the ABC Bill would come out of "general revenues" which are raised by general (federal) taxes on individuals. This leads to confusion as to whether an individual's taxes are going toward expenditures he or she favors. If taxpayers knew the actual price they paid for many government-provided services, they would not demand them. This is known as "fiscal illusion."[19]

Insofar as parents do feel that their costs of institutionalized child care have gone down, they will demand more of this kind of child care. Some argue that this "discriminates against traditional families where the mother is not employed."[20] It certainly may change the relative costs of the alternative ways that parents choose to care for their children, and therefore could increase the number of women entering the labor market.[21]

It should also be noted that parents, as a group, are very diverse and geographically dispersed. This means that they, as a lobbying group, will not be as effective as groups which are much less diverse. Therefore, even if many parents feel that child-care legislation is not in their best interest, the cost of organized lobbying may far outweigh tax costs. The only lobbying parents will be the ones that receive very strong emotional benefits from having their voices heard (such as mothers quoted in this paper).

Also important to note here is that the taxation to provide the increased funding for day care will be carried by *all* taxpayers; including those that do not use day care. As stated earlier, this does not mean that the legislation will necessarily target the poor at the expense of the rich (which is its intention).[22] On the contrary, in many cases higher-income families will use subsidized day care, while the lower-income families will not. Families with incomes of up to $48,000 annually would be eligible for subsidized day care. It appears that many low-income families do not use institutionalized day care. One source estimates that over 80 percent of children under the age of five in day care are from two-parent families in which both parents work outside of the home.[23] As would be apparent, the average income for these two-parent/two earner families is considerably higher than for those with only one earner.[24] Insofar as this is the case, low-income families would subsidize higher-income families if the ABC Bill goes into operation.

Finally, it is interesting to note also that among those that endorse the ABC Bill are several unions, including the Amalgamated Clothing and Textile Workers' Union and the International Ladies Garment Workers' Union. There could be two reasons for this support. First, many of the teachers, educators, or trainers which would be necessary to fill the needs of the ABC Bill are members of unions. The American Federation of Teachers, AFL-CIO and the Service Employees International Union, AFL-CIO are among the supporters of the bill.

On the other hand, even if those employees who compete with union members would be eligible to be hired to fill the needs of the bill (the bill specifically calls for training and technical assistance for child-care providers as well as an increase in salaries for child care providers), the relative salary differences between union employees and non-union employees would decrease. This would make the union employees relatively more attractive to employers.

The Losers

As stated earlier, clearly taxpayers will pay a great deal for the ABC legislation. The actual amount is impossible to determine. Those that use government-supported child-care services will be subsidized by those that do not.

Private day-care centers, businesses, and religious centers are eligible for the government funds. However, if they accept them, they will have to comply with the federal standards as set down by the government. Furthermore, religious institutions would not be able to discriminate on the basis of religion. Because of these reasons, many private day-care centers, businesses, and religious centers will not accept the federal funds. What that will mean is that they will be at a competitive disadvantage to those that do accept the funds insofar as the prices charged by the government-supported centers are lower.

An important consequence that seems to come about whenever an industry is characterized by both government-supported firms and private firms, is that the quality, even in the private firms, is lower than it otherwise might be. This is because insofar as private firms compete with government-supported firms, they are competing with different (usually lower) standards than if they were competing with other private firms. Therefore, since the government competition is of a different standard, private firms will also be able to supply at a different standard.

Insofar as private firms compete with one another, the market will still provide a wide range of standards as demanded by consumers. But one must keep in mind that these firms are always trying to meet consumer standards at a distinctive cost disadvantage. Consumers make their choices based upon relative price differences. Relatively high-priced private firms (which must charge the higher price in order to meet cost constraints and be competitive with government-subsidized firms) must be able to demonstrate to consumers that there is a large enough difference between the quality provided by the private firm and that provided by the government-subsidized firm to justify the price difference. Many private firms will not be able to do this and will either leave the market or decrease quality in order to decrease the price charged to consumers. The education industry is a good example. The day-care industry would follow the same pattern with the ABC Bill in place. Overall quality, in both government-subsidized and private day-care centers will probably decrease.

The Tax Credit Alternative

The proposed tax-credit alternative will have some differing consequences than that of the ABC Bill. This type of legislation is not as all-encompassing, and therefore would not increase the size of government by the same amount as the ABC Bill. Since it does not call for the need for such agencies as educational and training centers, data-collection bureaus, or referral programs, we do not see those existing agencies that fall into these categories lobbying for this type of legislation.

However, whenever the taxes of a special-interest group are decreased, unless government spending is also decreased, there is still a transfer of funds from the whole of society to this special-interest group. In this case the group is parents with children using institutionalized day care. Parents who want to have a greater choice as to how to use the money they would no longer pay in taxes will have much to gain from this type of legislation. The costs of the legislation are spread out among all taxpayers, while the benefits are accrued to the special-interest group.

An important aspect of a tax-credit bill such as the one introduced by Representative Schulze (H.R. 4434) is that it provides a "direct" subsidy to all families with incomes over $13,000 for each child under age six.[25] Families with incomes less than $8,000 a year would receive $15 for each $100 earned for one child under age six. For each additional child under age six, the parent would receive $10 for each $100 earned. For families between the income levels of $8,000 and $13,000 the bill would call for incremental reductions in the earned-income credit until the payment reached $5.75 for every $100 earned per child under age six.

This direct subsidy is important in that it would allow the parents of children under age six to choose exactly how they would spend the tax credit. Therefore, *all* types of child care, in essence, would be subsidized. This is in contrast to the ABC Bill under which institutionalized day care would be subsidized at the expense of non-institutionalized day care.

This could change the decisions of some women regarding whether or not they work in or outside of the home. It could also change the incentives of parents as to how many children they decide to have.

CONCLUSION

Certainly, with a tax-credit proposal there are fewer groups who can easily see a potential benefit to the legislation than with the ABC Bill. These groups include insurance companies, educational and research institutions, as well as unions. Therefore, proposals such as the tax-credit bills introduced will induce far less "rent-seeking"[26] behavior than legislation such as the ABC Bill.

What this means in terms of resource use is that far fewer resources are wasted when direct tax credits given to individuals themselves are proposed in the legislative process, as opposed to indirect subsidies which pinpoint very specific industries and/or firms that will be affected. Resources are wasted because rent-seeking is a negative-sum game.

> These expenditures (on rent seeking) add nothing to social
> product (they are zero-sum at best), and their opportunity
> cost constitutes lost production to society.[27]

However, both the ABC Bill and tax-credit proposals are designed to transfer wealth from the broad base of taxpayers in this country to those that have young children.[28] The costs and benefits of both proposing and implementing the two different types of legislation vary greatly. What individuals in our society must decide is whether or not subsidizing those with children at the expense of those without children is economically sound (does it really help those it intends to help?) and morally justified (is the loss in freedom that must accompany a larger government really worth it?).

—Deborah Walker is assistant professor of economics at Loyola University (New Orleans).

FOOTNOTES

[1]Buchanan, James M. and Gordon Tullock, *The Calculus of Consent* (Ann Arbor: The University of Michigan, 1965), p. 3.

[2]*Ibid.* See especially p. 4.

[3]This does not imply that someone other than an individual knows what is "best" for that individual. It only implies that if people knew the outcomes of their actions *ex ante*, they would, themselves, behave differently.

[4]All of the costs and benefits mentioned in this paper are subjective. Some are measurable in a monetary sense, but still valued differently by each individual.

[5]This bill was introduced by Senator Christopher Dodd (D- Conn.). A similar bill was introduced in the House by Representative Dale Kildee (D-Michigan) as H.R. 3660.

[6]Other tax credit proposals include H.R. 4434, "The Toddler Tax Credit," as S. 2620; and H.R. 3944, S. 2187, and H.R. 4768. The Bush proposal also includes an earned-income tax credit for very low income families.

[7]See for example, the testimonies of William Donald Schaefer, Governor of Maryland and Madeleine Kunin, Governor of Vermont.

[8]Niskanen, W.A. *Bureaucracy and Representative Government* (Chicago: Aldine Atherton, 1971).

[9]Testimony of Lawrence J. Schweinhart, High/Scope Educational Research Foundation, Subcommittee on Children, Family, Drugs and Alcoholism, Committee on Labor and Human Resources, U.S. Senate, January 24, 1989, Washington, D.C., p. 1.

[10]As mentioned, this does not suggest that private firms do not use the information provided by research institutions. Indeed, many of these institutions are privately funded. However, what is suggested is that the implementation of the ideas is very different in a market setting than in a non-market setting both because of the knowledge problem faced by all government agencies (see Boettke, Peter J. and Deborah Walker, "Knowledge Conveyance and Bureaucracy as an Economic Entity: Gordon Tullock and the Austrians on Economic Coordination," unpublished working paper, February 1989), and the incentive structure or agency problem of government agencies.

[11]Arthur R. Nielsen, Property and Casualty Group, CIGNA Corporation. Statement before the Subcommittee on Children, Family, Drugs and Alcoholism, Senate Committee on Labor and Human Resources on the Act for Better Child Care Services, Tuesday, January 24, 1989, pp. 4-5, emphasis added.

[12]See Hayek, Friedrich A. "The Meaning of Competition" in *Individualism and Economic Order* (Chicago: University of Chicago Press, 1948), p. 97.

[13]Klein, Benjamin and Keith B. Leffler, "The Role of Market Forces in Assuring Contractual Performance," *Journal of Political Economy*, vol. 89, no. 4 (1981): 615-641.

[14]Nelson, Phillip, "Advertising as Information," *Journal of Political Economy*, vol. 82, no. 4 (1974): 729- 754 and Nelson, Phillip, "Information and Consumer Behavior," *Journal of Political Economy*, vol. 78, no. 2 (1970): 311- 329.

[15]Statement of Mrs. Linda Hartshorn on the Act for Better Child Care Services before the U.S. Senate Labor and Human Resources Committee, Subcommittee on Children, Family, Drugs and Alcoholism, January 24, 1989, pp. 2-3. Emphasis in text.

[16]Testimony to the Subcommittee on Children and Youth by Cheri Robertson, January 24, 1989, p. 2.

[17]See Charles Murray, *Losing Ground: American Social Policy 1950-1980,* 1984 (New York: Basic Books, Inc.).

[18]Either through direct taxation or an inflation tax. The government could increase its deficit, of course, which is politically expedient. However, this too must eventually be paid for by future generations, in one form or another. Perhaps the children subsidized today will be forced to pay for their own child care in the future.

[19]Buchanan, James M., *Public Finance in a Democratic Process* (Chapel Hill: University of North Carolina Press, 1967). See p. 73. See also Wagner, Richard E. "Revenue Structure, Fiscal Illusion, and Budgetary Choice," *Public Choice* 25 (Spring 1976): 45-61.

[20]Rector, Robert. "The American Family and Day-Care," The Heritage Foundation *Issue Bulletin* No. 128, April 6, 1988, p. 19.

[21]This assumes that in most cases it is the mother who has the lower opportunity cost (relative to the father) of not working outside of the home.

[22]Rector, *op. cit.*

[23]The Bureau of the Census, U.S. Department of Commerce, "Who's Minding the Kids?" Household Economic Studies, Series P- 70, No. 9, May 1987. The data was collected between December 1984 and March 1985.

[24]According to the Bureau of the Census, the median income for two-earner families is $38,346, while it is only $25,803 for one-earner families. Bureau of the Census, 1987 figures.

[25]The tax credit is $750 per child. If the value of total tax credits exceeded tax liabilities, the difference would be refunded to the family.

[26]Rent-seeking, as defined by Robert Tollison is competition "for artificially contrived transfers." Artificially contrived because they do not arise through changes in the price system but through government action. See Tollison, Robert D., "Rent Seeking: A Survey," *Kyklos* 35 (1982): 575- 601.

[27]Ibid., p. 576.

[28]Government wealth transfers of any kind are not, in my opinion, economically or morally justified. However, that analysis is beyond the scope of this paper. Parental choice and better child care are provided in a strong economy. A strong economy is the answer to any "day care problem" parents may be facing.

Participants in Consultation on "The Economics of Day Care"

April 21, 1989

Authors of Papers

James Walker, assistant professor of economics, University of Wisconsin, Madison, Wisconsin.

Deborah Walker, assistant professor of economics, Loyola University, New Orleans, Louisiana.

Other Participants

Allan Carlson, president of The Rockford Institute, Rockford, IL.

Stephen Chapman, columnist, Chicago Tribune, Chicago, IL.

Bryce Christensen, director of The Rockford Institute Center on the Family in America, Rockford, IL.

Judith Finn, economic consultant, Eagle Forum, Arlington, VA.

Mary Kohler, Windway Capital Corporation, Sheboygan, WI.

Maurice MacDonald, professor of family economics, University of Wisconsin, Institute for Research on Poverty, Madison, WI.

Robert Rector, policy analyst, The Heritage Foundation, Washington, DC.

Richard Vedder, professor of economics, Ohio University, Athens, OH.

The Economics of Day Care:
Summary of a Discussion

E conomist and housewife, journalist and business executive, policy analyst and researcher—eleven spokesmen, drawn from different backgrounds, met together at The Sheraton International Hotel outside Chicago, Illinois in April 1989 to discuss the "economics of day care." As participants considered two papers written by Professor James Walker and Professor Deborah Walker (published in this volume), their exchange of views showed that economics—especially the economics of day care—cannot be considered wholly apart from social and cultural trends.

Acting as chairman for the consultation, Bryce Christensen opened the first session by surveying some of the pressures that have pushed day care into the public debate. He noted that as an increasing number of the mothers of young children have entered the workforce, the demand for day care has grown. Not all agree about the reasons that more young mothers are now in the labor force. Some believe this trend reflects the decline in what used to be called the family wage, a wage high enough to allow a man to support his wife and children. But others say that it is primarily a rising level of economic expectations, and not a real decline in male wages, which is putting more mothers into the work force. "Young people, it seems, want more—a condominium, two cars, two VCR's, a Caribbean vacation—and they want it sooner in life than their parents." For feminists, Christensen observed, "the primary question is that of ending wives' economic and social dependence upon their husbands, quite apart from whether their maternal employment actually enriches the household." The economic independence of women from husbands and the placement of children in group care have been features of utopian literature since Plato, he pointed out.

On the other hand, Christensen cautioned participants not to forget that about half the mothers of pre-schoolers do not work, while many who do work still arrange for a spouse or grandparents to care for their children. Young mothers often make great financial sacrifices to care for their own children. As new research—including that discussed at the December consultation— has exposed the psychological risks of day care, many working mothers have carried an increased burden of guilt and have wished their economic circumstances did not require their employment. Other employed mothers have called for government to invest more public money in day care to reduce the risks. Accordingly, measures are now being debated in Washington and in many state capitals for increasing the public support for day care. One approach (exemplified by the ABC Bill) would provide monies specifically to day-care centers and their clients. A second approach (supported by President Bush) would give special tax credits to parents of preschoolers, so giving working mothers more money for child care, but not discriminating against mothers who choose to stay home. In yet a third approach, government would require large companies to include day care with their benefit package. It was partly to clarify the debate over these initiatives that The Rockford Institute Center on The Family in America convened the consultation.

In presenting his paper, Professor James Walker explained that he was trying to develop "a neoclassical economic approach" to the household economy, to providing a model for interpreting the major trends in the use of day care. He stressed that his framework offered "a way of recognizing that child care . . . is costly," not only because of direct expenditures on food, clothing, and other goods, but also because of the time that a woman must devote to child care. Properly to understand the cost of child care, it is necessary to consider what economists call "opportunity cost," that is, the money that a woman forfeits if she chooses to care for her child rather than to enter paid employment. The decision to place a child in day care thus depends upon the parents' preferences or "tastes," the household's resources, the cost of child care, and the economic opportunities for a woman in the marketplace. Anything that increases the relative price of child care—such as an increase in women's wages or a decrease in the cost of market day care will tend to cause parents to choose day care.

Walker rejected the possibility of assessing the worth of child care by examining a single criterion. Rather, different households will seek different qualities—convenience, nurturance, hygiene, education—and will make choices in day care in ways comparable to the way that people buy new cars after comparing the features of different models. Consequently, the diversity in day care reflects a diversity in parental preferences.

Identifying "the most important insight" in his analysis, Walker emphasized that increasing use of day care is not simply *caused by* increasing maternal employment. Rather, rising female employment and rising use of day care are "jointly determined." The same forces which cause more young mothers to work also cause parents to place their children in day care. Many of these forces lie beyond the household's control. Walker noted that between 1970 and 1985, married women with children under the age of three increased their participation in the labor market from just 25 percent to slightly over 50 percent. Social scientists and economists have not yet determined all the reasons, but women are more willing to work than in the past, so increasing the demand for day care. Some see declining discrimination against female employment as a primary reason that more women have committed themselves to education and employment. By giving women greater control over their reproductive biology, contraception has also increased the incentive for women to pursue an education and to remain in the workplace.

In Walker's view, the rising level of female employment has also affected the demand for day care indirectly by reducing the number of female relatives—grandmothers and aunts—available to care for the children of a working mother. The possibility for a working mother to choose some arrangement other than day care has also been reduced by the mobility of modern households and by a general decline in the extended household. Walker also took note of how increasing marital instability has reduced the resources of the household and has removed the possibility for many mothers of sharing the burden of child care with a spouse.

Part-time and "flex time" schedules have had little effect upon the demand for day care, Walker observed, seeing little change in the work week for female employees over recent decades. On the other hand, government policies such as the income-tax credit for child care have significantly affected the incentives for using day care. Addressing the issue of corporate policy, Walker saw few incentives for companies to support day care, despite widespread advocacy of such support. Companies have been slow to develop day-care systems for their employees because corporate officials fear such systems will prove expensive, while meeting the needs of relatively few employees. Besides, given the dramatic increase in female employment over the past 15 years, it appears as though employers do not need to offer day care in order to attract capable women.

Serving as the discussant for James Walker's paper, Richard Vedder praised Professor Walker for developing "a comparatively simple but effective way" to explain how changes in relative prices of household goods and services can explain changes in the use of day care. "Changes in the price of nonmaternal day care, relative to mother-provided care, are an important part of the story of the changing role of the American family," Vedder affirmed. Vedder also lauded Walker's paper for its identification of the technological revolution in the household and the establishment in 1976 of an income-tax credit for child care as important parts of the explanation of the growth of nonparental day care.

Yet Vedder confessed that in reading Professor Walker's paper, he was "struck by some other questions that were not fully discussed." Why, for instance, has the labor-force participation of those with small children risen so dramatically compared to the labor-force participation of other women? Such a pattern raises "the more basic question of motivation": "Are the motivations that have led increasing proportions of mothers with small children to work and to entrust their children to others," asked Vedder, "the same motivations that have led women to have fewer births in the first place?"

On another point, Vedder expressed doubt about whether Professor Walker had provided an "adequate economic explanation for the failure of part-time female employment to grow relative to full-time employment." Perhaps, he conjectured, the costs of training part-time workers and of paying for their fringe benefits are sufficiently large to make their employment "prohibitively expensive" for employers. Public policy may also discourage such employment he suggested.

Agreeing with Walker that changing family structure has affected demand for day care, Vedder reasoned that these changes in family structure might partly be traced to changes in public policy which have reduced the relative costs of becoming an unwed or divorced mother. Some would argue that "incentives to divorce have grown over time because of the unintended consequences of public policy." Such issues, Vedder suggested, could be investigated using the framework Walker deployed in his paper.

Vedder disputed Walker's assertion that working mothers had to rely on day care because fewer female relatives were available to provide care. The one group of women for whom labor-force participation has not risen materially since 1970 is those over 55, he pointed out, so that "the number of non-working women from 55 to 64 actually grew an impressive 21 percent from 1970 to 1986." "The number of [unemployed] grandmothers was growing faster than the number of small kids," Vedder remarked. "Grandmothers may not be caring as much for children as earlier, but it is not primarily because grandmothers have abandoned their homes for work." Vedder called for more research into this issue, wondering, particularly how the rapid improvement of the economic status of elderly Americans has affected their role in caring for their grandchildren.

In conclusion, Vedder offered "five bits of casual empiricism" that may suggest that "Americans today simply don't like children as much as they used to." First, fertility is nearly at an all time low, while abortion is probably at an historically high level. Second, "American mothers probably spend less time with what few children they have than at any other time in our nation's history." Third, "the ratio of poor children to poor old persons has risen dramatically in the last generation [but] no one seems terribly interested in doing anything about it. Poverty among children is up, yet poverty among people over 65 is down." Four, the schools are "widely perceived to be preparing children inadequately for both the moral and economic challenges in the coming century." Fifth, "Crime, drug addiction, and even suicide among teenagers are at near-record highs. The ability of children to assimilate in civilized society with a rule of law is perhaps less now than at any time in modern history." All of these developments, he suggested, could partially reflect changing public policies. "Over time, the growth of government has increased the relative importance of public-policy decisions. Children are uniquely disadvantaged in the public-policy arena: adults vote, children don't." As someone who had worked on Capitol Hill, Vedder sensed a "general anti-children atmosphere" in Washington, D.C. where Congressmen are "notorious for their neglect of their own children." "Government," he speculated, "may be inherently anti- child and the increase in government's relative importance may contribute to the deterioration in child status."

Deborah Walker entered the conversation expressing concern about the social assumptions underlying James Walker's focus on the relationship between child care and *female* labor force participation. The question should be reframed to consider *both* male and female labor force participation, she urged.

James Walker responded that his simplifying assumption that the husband would not be responsible for child care was "purely expositional," not prescriptive. He conceded that child-care decisions would actually be "jointly determined" by the employment decisions of both parents.

Mary Kohler challenged the judgment, found in James Walker's paper, that day care poses few risks for children. In attending the December consultation on day care (also summarized in this volume), she had learned of a number of medical and psychological problems linked to day care. Kohler also voiced doubts about the reference in James Walker's paper to "large cut backs in Federal subsidy for publicly supplied day care." Rather she argued that the amount of the subsidy had not decreased but that projected increases had been cut.

James Walker resisted this opinion, noting actual cuts in Title XX funding for day care, though some additional monies (under drug abuse prevention) had been directed to Head Start and teacher training.

Robert Rector found it misleading to assess public support for day care merely by looking at Title XX funds, which had been cut, but not dramatically. If tax credits given to working women for day care are counted as a public expenditure, then Federal funding for day care has not declined.

The question of cutbacks in day-care funding need to be examined specifically for the low-income population, Maurice MacDonald remarked. James Walker agreed, pointing out that since low-income families don't have taxable income, a tax credit for day care has no value *for them*. On the other hand, cuts in Title XX funds for day care do affect their day-care costs. A shift in public day-care policy away from direct subsidy toward tax credits has the decided effect of shifting benefits away from low-income families.

Attempting to draw out the issues thematically, Allan Carlson asserted that the economic analysis is premised upon individual choice rather than upon household integrity. The focus, in his view, should be on the household. To place the day-care debate in its historical context, Carlson cited the work of Charlotte Perkins Gilman, who 80 years ago discerned a "long term economic trend" toward "the steady surrender by the household of its economic functions to the marketplace." Even in the early 1900's, Gilman was able to show that in the urban and suburban setting, "the emerging world of America," almost all of the family's economic functions had been transferred to the marketplace, with only three exceptions: food, cleaning services, and child care. Because of the public-school movement, even child care had to some degree been transferred out of the home. As Gilman called for a completion of the process, a battle broke out between those who shared her unlimited faith in market efficiency and those who wanted to defend what came to be called "the traditional home." Defenders of the traditional family feared that the family would disintegrate as a meaningful unit of economic activity if any more of its functions were transferred to the market. Yet as Gilman looked to the future, she anticipated some actual developments. She looked to a time when families would not eat at home but instead in clean, efficient shops, vaguely like McDonalds. While both parents worked, child-care experts would care for children in places that sound remarkably like Kindercare, Inc. Finally, Gilman foresaw the replacement of home cleaning by professional cleaning services, now one of the fastest growing segments of the service economy. In order to understand the changing economics of day care, Carlson observed it is necessary to see the "larger pattern" sketched out by Gilman. The rise of day care means that the home is "losing its last productive activity." While "certain efficiencies" may be gained in this shift, he doubted whether day-care workers could provide the same kind of individual attention, love, and discipline that parents can. Carlson judged the long range prospects for children "very poor."

Warming to Carlson's line of analysis, Vedder traced the pattern back much farther than Gilman. Centuries ago, he stressed, "virtually all production took place in the family." The movement away from the family as an independent economic unit, a unit of production, has developed as part of a very long historical process. With the rise of day care, modern America reaches the ultimate conclusion of this process. "The last gasp of the family is at hand. . . . The family is ceasing to have any function of a direct economic nature," he concluded.

For James Walker, this scenario seemed a bit extreme. People are not about to form large households based on "comparative advantage" and designed to produce "scale economics." After all, there are still some "attributes within our families that we cannot get anywhere else: the love, the care, the affection, the concern—these things that we can't substitute away from."

But Bryce Christensen reported that, according to a recent history of prostitution, contemporary streetwalkers can scarcely make a living because so many women are now willing to engage in casual sex. An increasing number of people do appear willing to seek intimacy outside marriage and family, even if not in the marketplace.

MacDonald believed some natural limit exists for the process of replacing family functions with marketplace systems. Indeed, he said that individuals are afraid to move to another phase in this process. Government action could prove decisive in determining whether Americans reach some sort of social equilibrium or whether those trends away from family life continue. For those convinced that further movement away from the family is inevitable, the market can be allowed to do its work independently, free from government intrusion. But among those who believe that society has a long way to go, some will agree that government should speed up the process by subsidizing more day care. Confessing uncertainty about where we are in the economic shift away from family life and how much farther we may go, he asked Allan Carlson for an opinion.

In his response, Carlson discerned a domestic compromise reached by Americans in the late 19th century, when they had purposefully set limits on the intrusion of the market into the home. Americans had set barriers, some legal, some cultural, defining child care and care of the home as noneconomic activities. But he agreed with MacDonald about the importance of government policy in affecting home life. Government support of day care has helped drive up the relative cost of caring for children at home and to push down the relative cost of day care. Citing the work of Reuben Gronau on the value of home production, Carlson noted that it still makes no economic sense for the mother of a preschooler to begin market work at the median female income, because of all the things that she can no longer do for the family. Acknowledging that the market does "push" on the boundaries of home life, Carlson expressed faith in "instinctive human desires to stop it at certain places." But problems arise when these instincts are thwarted by government leaders who start manipulating the economic incentives for ideological reasons.

Surveying current fertility levels, MacDonald saw evidence of the kind of fundamental human instincts referred to by Carlson. MacDonald conceded that fertility is low now, but emphasized that it is stable and "not vanishing." Americans could escape the whole economic problem that children create by not bearing any, but that is not happening. Childbearing still means something to people.

More pessimistic, Carlson said that while parents might sacrifice to bear a first child, who will give them love and affection, they are less likely to do so for a second child, who — after all—can offer only "a marginal addition of love."

Perhaps, MacDonald conceded, that is why most people are now having only two children instead of three or four. Yet MacDonald persisted in interpreting the willingness to bear even one child as evidence of humane impulses not reducible to economics. Such impulses, he reiterated, make it hard to accept a simple extrapolation of economic trends away from family life.

But while MacDonald clung to evidence that people build families despite economic pressure, Stephen Chapman wanted to know why so many mothers go to work even when they find no economic advantage in doing so. Is it possible, Chapman asked, that work, or family, or society have changed in ways that make raising children less satisfying than it used to be?

The evidence appeared mixed to Rector. He noted that while between 70 and 80 percent of mothers still state that they would prefer to remain at home with their children when finances permit, it is hard to tell how much they are willing to sacrifice economically in order to rear their own children. Having represented full-time mothers frequently in public debates, Rector had heard them frequently complain of the intense pressure that results from the cultural devaluation of traditional mothering. Many of these women feel that they are under a cultural assault, bombarded by mass media telling them that what they are doing is "antediluvian" or "menial labor of little real value." Rector himself discovered this prejudice in Washington, where no one would believe him when he cited statistics showing that the majority of preschool children are still being raised at home. Despite the validity of these statistics, Congressmen would literally sneer in disbelief, convinced that all children either are in day-care centers or that their parents want to place them in such centers. Rector did hold out hope that antimaternal bias may be easing up, perhaps in part because many mothers of young children have questioned the relative value of a second income. Disputing James Walker's assessment of part-time employment, Rector noted that many mothers who work full time do so only part of the year. Only about a third of preschoolers have mothers who work full-time year round. Given women's distinctive employment patterns, Rector conjectured that if tax policies were designed to raise the net income of the primary earner, more women would work fewer hours or cease paid employment altogether.

Vedder wanted to know the age distribution of the mothers who worked full-time intermittently, hypothesizing that mothers with school-age children would be more interested in working full-time during the school year but being home during the summer. This pattern, he noted, underscored the fact that "schools are ultimately a form of day care." "No one questions day care above the age of five, except we call it school." At a time when some advocate school for four-and three-year-olds, educational issues have become an extension of the day-care debate.

As several participants raised questions about statistical patterns, Chapman found evidence of a significant increase in the number of women without children, especially without small children, who are now working full time, year round.

James Walker stressed that the choice of full- or part-time employment depends not only on individual preference but also on market demand for labor. An employer's costs in hiring two part-time workers rather than one full-time worker may discourage him from hiring part-time workers. Yet because those intent upon working part-time will probably accept lower wages, in the long run part-time jobs should open up. Arguably, we are now in a "transitional period" as employers and working parents sort things out.

Shifting the discussion, Carlson noted that the rise in the percentage of women in the labor market has been paralleled by a decline in percentage of men of all ages who are employed. Taken together, this pattern reflects what might be called "the decline or collapse of the family wage concept." Carlson also commented on the oddity of the extremely high rate of employment among mothers with preschoolers, a rate of employment even higher than among women with older children.

Vedder underscored this point, contrasting the current pattern with the very different picture in 1970 when women with older children were more likely to be employed than women with preschoolers. James Walker explained that this trend is strongly linked to the age of the women employed, regardless of whether these women are mothers of preschoolers.

Understanding the recent shift in maternal employment, Carlson suggested, requires a consideration of broader issues. In Sweden, for example, no group—male or female, young or old— reports a higher employment rate than the mothers of preschool children. This odd employment pattern, which has appeared quite recently and could not be seen twenty years ago, developed partly as the result of economic pressures, but largely as the result of ideological forces that won passage of public policies designed to foster such a situation.

But James Walker hastened to add a footnote indicating that much of the recent rise of employment for Swedish women has been in part-time work, especially for local government, which has mushroomed in the last two decades.

At the risk of sounding either "terribly reactionary or terribly Marxist," Carlson ventured that part of the reason that Americans have retreated from child-rearing is not that they like children less but that over the past 40 or 50 years Americans have "stripped children of their direct economic value to their parents and turned them into just enormously expensive consumption goods." Specifically, Carlson identified Social Security as a system which collectivizes care between the generations, so taking this economic responsibility away from the family and turning it over to the government. Children are no longer the "insurance policies" they were for parents before 1940. On the other hand, the enactment of Child Labor Laws has sharply restricted the possibility that children can make a major contribution to the family economy, especially for lower-class households.

To put the investigation in a different light, James Walker challenged the premises of those labor economists who view American employment patterns in the 1980's as anomalous and the pattern in the 1950's—when most women were staying home—as the norm. Perhaps the 1950's were the anomaly, while recent years have seen a return to the long-term norm. Before this century, when most Americans lived on farms, women shared the family's economic burdens by working in the fields, maintaining the household, and caring for children. Not only was child care relatively inexpensive, parents wanted children to help with farm labor. After the Industrial Revolution, after child-labor laws and the rise of public education, the relative cost of child-rearing rose. Still, Walker found it difficult to give a strictly economic explanation for recent employment and fertility trends. Changing attitudes about the proper role for women also influenced decisions. The total effect, however, has not been to reduce the number of families that ever have a child but to reduce the likelihood of a third or fourth child. In both the United States and Sweden, over 90 percent of all women will still bear at least one child, and most will bear a second as well, though fewer will now have a third, perhaps because of the changes in the relative cost of children.

Offering a different perspective, Christensen referred to *Corruption in Paradise: The Child in Western Literature* by Reinhard Kuhn. In looking at high literature, Kuhn established two things: 1) that— —contrary to the views of some historians, such as Philippe Ariès — parents felt a deep affection for their children in pre-industrialized Europe; 2) that a door has shut on children in modern literature. Christensen ventured that if the poet can transcend economics and sociology, then this literary contrast signals a decisive change in cultural ideals. Christensen found it especially noteworthy that modern literature had turned away from children despite the Baby Boom.

James Walker admitted his inability to respond to the literary argument. He conceded the importance of new cultural pressures and changing gender roles, but still maintained that economic forces could account for much of the decline in fertility. As a possible counterargument to those who say Americans value children less than in the past, he proposed that Americans want "higher quality" children, so we have fewer but spend more on each.

Judith Finn would not trust the economic argument very far to explain why people pass up parenthood for employment. Young people are actually better off economically than parents typically were in any previous generations. "Our whole understanding of what children need has changed," she declared. This is now discussed in terms of money for college, lessons, and day care, rather than nurturing and shaping in a stable family.

The movement of women into the labor force not only was a *consequence* of economic change, Kohler reminded participants, but it was also a *cause* of economic change. As the number of two-earner households have multiplied, "the rich have gotten richer and the poor have gotten poorer." When both husband and wife hold good jobs, the number of jobs available to others is naturally reduced. Given this exacerbated inequality of income, well-to-do households and poor households must base their family lives on quite different economic assumptions. Yet, with Finn, Kohler believed that changes in culture have had a very strong impact on child-rearing decisions.

While identifying herself as a woman with "no desire whatsoever to stay at home with children," Deborah Walker decried the negative stereotype of the homemaker. What is needed, Walker argued, are policies which foster stigma-free personal choice and defuse the animosity between traditionalists and nontraditionalists.

Yet some of that animosity flared into view when Walker concluded with the assertion that it is "economically good for a man to be married and economically bad for a woman to be married." Kohler strongly denied that claim, alleging that married women are better off economically. Walker explained that she meant that while married men earn more than single men, married women earn less than single women. Because they perform domestic duties not generally done by men, married women cannot earn as much as their male counterparts.

Rector entered the fray, arguing that higher-earning males are more likely to marry than low-earning men. Once married, men feel greater financial pressure than non-married men and therefore devote themselves to more work and accept more difficult assignments. For married women, the exact opposite is likely to occur.

Deborah Walker countered that a man can devote more time to the labor market once he is married precisely because his wife does many things for him.

Chapman tried to adjudicate the dispute by conjecturing that men and women respond to marriage differently. Once married, men will tell themselves that they must work harder. For many women on the other hand, marriage means that other responsibilities should take priority over paid employment. The diverging attitudes will naturally affect intensity of effort, commitment to the job, job continuity, and related matters.

Deborah Walker disavowed any interest in trying to coerce men and women from making these kinds of choices. But she hoped individual choices could be liberated from biases, traditional and anti-traditional.

Still skeptical, Kohler worried that children would be hurt by "too much individual choice," since children's desires are not consulted when everything is predicated on personal preference rather than the good of society.

"What is society?" asked Deborah Walker. "Who is going to decide what is good for society?"

Sidestepping these questions, Rector returned to the problems created because children have no voice in shaping policy. Although attracted to a policy which encourages individual choice, he felt it important to keep in mind the future of children. Rector feared the consequences for that future if children were increasingly placed in institutional settings such as day care. "I can't think of a more stultifying way to raise children," he opined.

Deborah Walker denied that she was trying to deprive children of their rights. Children are individuals, too, she recognized.

Tongue in cheek, MacDonald proposed that the time had come to enfranchise children.

In the same facetious spirit, Rector proposed a poll of preschoolers on the ABC Day-Care Bill to see if they would favor a government policy that discourages their mothers from staying at home to take care of them. Lacking hard scientific data, Rector was willing to make a leap of faith on the outcome of such a poll.

But what if the same imaginary pollsters asked young children if their fathers should leave home to work? queried James Walker. Children don't want to see their dads go to work either. The point, Judith Finn interrupted, is that preschool children don't want to see *both* parents go to work. "They may not want to see either one of them go, but they certainly don't want to see both of them go."

Returning to the earlier debate over whether Americans now care for children as much as in the past, Vedder intuited that people have "the same innate love for children that they always have had. That is one of the great constants of history." Now, however, children have become a consumer good. Even by 1950, children had largely ceased to be an economic asset, since few children were working on farms in the mid-20th century. Possibly, the cost of child-rearing has risen compared to the cost of airfares, personal computers, and other forms of consumer goods that also provide satisfaction in our lives. "We are trading in children for BMW's, and when we have children we want BMW children not Chevette children."

Vedder encouraged a rethinking of the evidence (previously cited by Carlson) showing that the employment of mothers of small children was not economically rational. The question of economic rationality, Vedder reasoned, depends on who you ask and whether economic benefits are assessed for the household or for the individual mother or father. *Someone* benefits when the mother goes to work, Vedder posited. Maybe the benefits of maternal employment have risen because of government action, he observed. Mothers also find emotional advantages in employment not there in the past. "Fifteen or twenty years ago, people felt guilty about going to work. Today, they feel guilty about staying home." Mothers who went to work in the past worried that their kids were being deprived. Now, mothers who stay home feel like "some sort of crazy who's out of tune with modern society."

The analysis outlined by Vedder did not fully satisfy Chapman. If kids were some type of "inferior good," then richer people would have fewer of them, just as rich people spend less on potatoes than poor people. Chapman found it odd that as income rises, Americans bear fewer children. But he noted that this was nothing new. As Americans have grown steadily richer for the last two hundred years, the fertility rate has dropped steadily—*except* during the twenty years after World War II. "*That* is the anomaly," Chapman insisted. "That is what takes explaining."

In Jim Walker's view, understanding the economics of family life required a closer examination of the division of resources within the household. Who makes financial decisions? Is it the individual? The household? How do we make decisions in the household? If we have children, what kind of resources do we expend on these children? Economists can measure a family's income without knowing how resources will be devoted to children. Perhaps, Walker conjectured,

American parents are spending less time with their children and instead giving their offspring video and computer games and other often expensive things that presumably enrich their lives. No one wants to say that children are "inferior goods" that adults will not want as their wealth increases, yet as real wealth has risen in this century, fertility has fallen. Some analysts therefore advance the argument that Americans now demand "quality children."

Falling mortality rates might partly account for lower fertility rates, Chapman commented. "People are having fewer kids now because they know all their kids are going to live. Fifty or one hundred years ago, they knew some of their kids would not survive to adulthood."

James Walker wondered about the applicability of this argument, though, given the relative stability of infant mortality rates since shortly after World War II.

Turning to a statement in an earlier version of James Walker's paper, Rector challenged the argument that the welfare reform of 1988 would create new demands for day care. In its full implementation in the mid 1990's, that bill requires only 12-13 percent of all welfare mothers to be involved in a job search or in training. Every state can meet that requirement without requiring the participation of any mothers of preschoolers. In any case, Rector did not expect to see the workfare goals met by 1995. As someone who had worked on workfare for more than ten years, Rector did not expect to see any appreciable improvement in his lifetime. Politicians may be expected to talk about putting welfare mothers to work, but they will not follow through. At the time the welfare reform bill was enacted, Rector said he had predicted that although the measure would *not* put welfare mothers of preschoolers into the workforce, the reform *would* be used as a pretext for building government day-care centers that would actually be used by working and middle-class households. The speed with which his prediction had been fulfilled astonished him.

Looking more broadly at the day-care debate, Rector identified seven variables — all laid out in James Walker's paper — essential to an understanding of the issue. First are the taxes on the primary earner. Second are the taxes on the secondary earner. The third are day-care subsidies. The fourth is the wage rate of the mother relative to that of the father. The fifth are changes in tastes. Sixth are rising financial expectations (actually a type of change in tastes). And seventh is the technology of home production. Rector especially stressed rising financial expectations. Because of this shift in what Americans regard as a normal standard of living, valid arguments that families are in fact better off financially than they were in the 1950's are heatedly rejected.

Rector also emphasized the importance of the tax rate on the father's income. Today, Federal taxes consume about 24 percent of the income of an average family of four, compared to only 2 percent in the early 1950's. Since the average mother contributes 32 percent of total family income, it is arguable that the labor force participation of women has merely compensated for the increased share of family income diverted to the Federal government.

Still, despite the earlier discussion of the economic rationality of maternal employment, Rector suspected—on the basis of Wendy Dreskin's *The Daycare Decision*—that many families don't make financial calculations prior to committing the mother to the work-force. Rather, many couples unthinkingly imitate what everybody else is doing. Many families end up boxing themselves into decisions that, in retrospect, they regret. For instance, a couple, influenced by a contemporary culture which assumes that no parent could want to stay home, may saddle themselves with a huge mortgage that requires two paychecks, only to discover that that decision looks quite different once a baby is born. Rector held out hope that parents might start to make better choices as they become better informed.

MacDonald could not believe that large numbers of mothers are locked into employment because of short-sighted mistakes. Perhaps this happens to some, but over time most people can back out of such situations, if they want to. MacDonald counted cultural pressure as an important cause of maternal employment. He speculated that poets had stopped writing about children because of the rise of indi-vidualism. During the 1950's, a cultural movement emerged to escape mass society. At-home mothers are now on the other side of that movement. Accordingly, we have the curious phenomenon that now the rebels are the traditional people while before the rebels were antitraditionalists.

Interjecting a comment on corporate policy, Kohler reported the case of a large corporation that set up a day-care facility in their plant only to discover that employees preferred day care near their homes so that both father and mother could easily pick up or drop off a child. For smaller companies, Kohler judged day care an even less practical idea. Kohler saw more promise in the possibility of including day care as one option in a flexible benefits package.

Finn conceded the reality of economic pressure on families; yet, she persisted in the belief that most mothers who are sufficiently determined can remain home to care for their own children. "What is happening," she worried, "is that kids really aren't the central concern of mothers, a dramatic change indeed." Finn argued that we don't like to admit that most women must choose either to have a career and maximize their economic potential or to make their children the center of their lives. The challenge to the perception that women should make children their central concern is more fundamental than economic pressure.

In the same vein, Rector thought it curious that at exactly the same time that American culture was telling women that in order to be fulfilled human beings they had to have careers, some psychologists generated a body of research saying essentially that industrialized child-rearing is as good as Mom. Rector judged that research to be "the greatest insult to mothers that has ever been put forward." In his own conversations with day-care center operators, Rector found that—aside from those highly politicized—few would assert anything like that.

Returning to the political debate over day care, Rector detected a peculiar but implicit argument in many of the discussions in Washington, where many analysts assume that since an unemployed mother pays no taxes, a truly "neutral" government policy would permit an employed mother to pay no taxes, perhaps even to receive some rebate on her husband's taxes through a day-care subsidy. This, Rector protested, is certainly not a neutral government policy. This kind of governmental policy adds to the overall fiscal pressure that tends to push mothers into the labor force.

While tax policy defined the topic, Allan warned that in the future American taxation might move toward "the big step" Sweden took in 1971, when the government moved from the taxation of the household to the taxation of individuals. This step—taken for very explicit reasons—represented "the triumph of feminism over socialism" and caused pronounced effects on people's wages. The fundamental question remains: What is the unit of society? Individual or family?

The total tax system needs assessment, according to James Walker, who pointed out that not only do families pay taxes, they also receive benefits from those taxes, including everything from B1 bombers to transportation systems, better schools, and student loans. Rector thought that, on balance, the family was asked to sacrifice too much for the benefits received.

Vedder cited the statistical evidence in *The Family Wage: Work, Gender, and Children in the Modern Economy* (published by The Rockford Institute in 1988) showing that the traditional family does face greater financial pressures than in the past. After taking taxes and welfare assistance into account, the single-earner family has suffered some deterioration in relative economic status. Vedder also suspected that the increased labor-force involvement of women, especially younger women, could largely account for the rise in income inequality in America over the past 20 to 25 years.

Concluding the first session of the constitution on a philosophic note, Christensen tried to explain both the fall in fertility and rising economic expectations as consequences of a pervasive myth of immortality. Drawing upon the work of Philippe Ariès, he noted how death is denied, suppressed, pushed out of view in modern Western culture. In contrast, the contemplation of death was traditionally encouraged as spiritually and morally beneficial. Perhaps immortals don't need to bear children, but meditation upon death leads to thoughts both of ancestors and of posterity. "Death is the strongest rebuke to the myth of individualism," Christensen said. Reflection upon death also curbs materialism by reminding us that we never "get ahead in life," since we take nothing with us. Christensen endorsed an observation by George Orwell (an unbeliever) who once cautioned that as Christianity declined, there was a strong temptation to console oneself with some optimistic illusion. People pursue material goods rather than bear children in part because they are living in the myth of individual immortality.

To open the second session, Professor Deborah Walker explained in outline the public-choice premises upon which her paper was written. Public-choice economists, she explained, apply the basic principles of economics to political activity. "The same assumptions that we make about people acting in the market, we make about people acting in the political arena." This perspective offers a somewhat cynical view of government, she admitted, because of its stress upon self-interest. Within public-choice analysis, the only reason people may act differently in the political arena is that the institutional arrangements are different than in the market and so their incentives will be accordingly shifted. Public-choice analysts acknowledge that while people act in their own self interest, they sometimes make mistakes because of lack of information about the consequences of those choices. In particular, Walker suggested that although she had no desire to make their decisions for them, she wondered if parents would support a national day-care policy if they had more information about costs.

In looking at proposed day-care policies, Deborah Walker focused particularly on the ABC Bill and tax-credit policies. In analyzing both bills, she tried to identify "rent-seeking" behavior among those who would benefit or lose through the passage of each. Because the ABC Bill is much more complicated and would authorize more government growth, public-choice theory would predict that it would cause more rent-seeking behavior, as is indeed the case. Walker enumerated several groups trying to win passage for this measure because in some way they would benefit from it. Aside from children and parents, the first group to benefit from passage of the ABC Bill would be state officials. Hence, the motive for governors and other state politicians pushing for the measure. Walker outlined briefly the statutory formula—based on the number of children under age five, the number of low-income families, and the number of children receiving free lunch—for ABC benefits, arguing that these numbers for a particular state would affect a governor's zeal for ABC.

The second group Deborah Walker saw lobbying for ABC were representatives of educational agencies. As public agencies that see their budgets grow under ABC, such groups naturally rally to its support. Because the ABC bill would increase the demand for expert opinion, credentialed experts have an economic motive for supporting the bill. It is much easier to sell expert opinion to government institutions or to government-regulated institutions than it is to sell it on the open market.

Insurance groups constitute the third group of advocates for the ABC. Walker explained that insurance companies welcome Federal standards because such standards reduce the policing costs of insuring centers. Insurance underwriters can reduce their companies' fiscal responsibilities by including in their contracts a provision stating that they will not be liable for any mishap that occurs in a center in violation of Federal standards.

Parents define yet another group advocating passage of ABC, Walker noted, apologizing that she had not considered the bill from the children's perspective. Because they neither vote nor testify in congressional hearings, they do not fit well within a public-choice analysis. Even parents are so diverse, unorganized, and dispersed that they hardly form a lobbying group. Those parents who do testify are typically those finding some emotional benefit in so doing—parents of a child killed or injured in day care, for instance. Such parents demand government standards to increase the quality of child care. Some ask government to take responsibility away from

them as parents in making sure that day care is safe. Walker conjectured that these parents might not favor the ABC Bill if they knew
that its probable outcome would be a decline, not an improvement, in
day care, since the ABC would reduce all the market mechanism that
help to ensure quality. Parents may also be misguided in their support of ABC in that they are misinformed about the cost. When a
service is paid for out of general tax funds, users of that service often
fall into "fiscal illusion," not knowing the true cost of the service. If
parents had to pay for this service on the market, perhaps they would
not demand it at the price paid indirectly through government.

Union support for ABC somewhat puzzled Deborah Walker. She
ventured that perhaps unions support the measure because it would
subsidize salaries for day-care workers, so decreasing the gap
between union and nonunion wages, making union employees more
attractive.

Identifying the losers under the ABC bill, Deborah Walker first
named private day-care centers, many of which would be driven out
of the market by Federal standards. Religious day-care centers
would also suffer under ABC because they would have to sacrifice
some of their autonomy to receive benefits.

In a brief look at the tax credit alternative, Deborah Walker could
offer no catalogue of rent-seeking groups, since this approach to the
day-care issue is simpler, involving fewer groups. Still, she pointed
out that whenever taxes are reduced for any special-interest group,
income is redistributed from all of society to that group, unless the
tax cut is tied to a commensurate decrease in government spending.
The tax-cut alternative, however, would give parents more choice in
child-rearing by subsidizing all types of childrearing rather than simply institutionalized day care. Warning that rent-seeking is intrin-
sically a "negative sum game," Walker concluded by deploring the
waste of resources trying to win passage for the ABC Bill.

As discussant for Professor Walker's paper, Rector praised the
analysis for identifying some of the special interests driving the issue.
As someone who lives inside the Washington Beltway, though, he
complained that in her attitude toward the political process, Walker
was far too benign and optimistic. Rector marveled at the level of
banality, crudeness, and mendacity in contemporary politics. While
endorsing most of Walker's analysis of the winners under ABC, he
did offer two corrections. First, he thought it unlikely that state politicians would be swayed much in their enthusiasm for the ABC by the
statistical formula for benefits. Such calculations are simply too

arcane for a politician, he said—except perhaps once the bill has been passed. The mental vistas of most congressmen, he lamented, are defined by such things as *Parade Magazine*, a Sunday-supplement written at a comic-book level.

Beyond this problem, Rector underscored the importance of ideology. At a time when incumbent congressmen rarely lose an election, they feel little pressure for "vote-buying" legislation. To understand congressmen's attitudes toward day care, it is essential to consider their vision of society and the way they would like society to go.

Because politics is "a branch of theater," Rector explained, politicians must regularly engage in symbolic theatrical activity: they must go out and slay dragons over and over again. Half in jest, he proposed allowing government programs to lapse periodically so politicians could win credit for reinventing the same thing over and over again. The ABC Bill in particular is essentially Title XX all over again, but with Federal standards added.

Reviewing the ranks of those supporting ABC, Rector pointed first to the day-care providers, who are eager for the money the bill would give them. Child-development professionals, on the other hand, support ABC less for economic gain than for power. Such professionals can control child-rearing more fully when the child-rearing is institutional rather than parental. But since quality day care of the sort these experts prescribe would cost about $6,000 a year per child, families would be much better off if they were simply given even a small fraction of that money in cash and allowed to spend it as they will. Clearly, the day-care program being advocated by many professionals is not something families would voluntarily select.

Union support for ABC held no mystery for Rector. Since that bill includes a provision for a quasi-teacher certificate for day-care workers, a child-development associate degree, it appears that the National Education Association (NEA) intends to elevate day care to the status of an auxiliary to the public school system so that all of the many female day-care workers can be unionized.

Allied with the groups with a clear economic stake in the day-care issue, Rector saw a considerable number of "fellow travelers" with no financial motive. Such fellow travelers would include the PTA, the Junior League, the Association of Pediatricians. Since day care has been implicated in the spread of many diseases, Rector invoked a "theory of imprinting" to explain why even doctors with a profound disincentive to support ABC support it nonetheless. According to the theory of imprinting, a young duck is imprinted with the image of the first creature it sees—usually its mother—upon birth and follows it thereafter. In the behavior of many fellow-traveling groups, lining up behind the ABC Bill, Rector discerned "the imprint of a certain liberal ideology that the key to human happiness is an increase in public-sector expenditure."

Rector faulted Deborah Walker for looking too favorably upon what the ABC bill would actually do for parents. From his perspective, the ABC Bill creates a sharp dichotomy of interests, giving benefits to the social-service industry at the expense of parents in the rest of society. He then began ticking off all the preschool children who would *not* receive benefits under ABC: The 54 percent of preschool children who do not have employed mothers, the 4 percent of preschoolers with mothers who do paid work in their homes, the 7 percent of children who have tag-team parents, working different shifts so that one parent is always home with the children, the 11 percent of preschoolers cared for by grandparents, aunts, and other relatives. Overall, 76 percent of preschool children are in the care of parents or relatives. Of the remaining 24 percent, half are in unlicensed, informal neighborhood care, not covered under ABC. Only about one preschool child in ten is currently in a licensed day-care facility. Even for licensed day care, the ABC coverage is selective, offering funding to church-based day care (one third of all centers) only if they engage in no religious activity. Private, for-profit day-care centers (almost half of all centers) also receive second-class treatment in ABC's allocation of funds. Under ABC, almost all money would go to those quasi-governmental institutions now receiving Title XX funds. Not surprisingly, for-profit day-care providers regard ABC as a way of driving them out of business and have therefore formed a coalition against it.

Taxpayers would head the list of losers under the ABC bill, Rector said. But the 9 out of 10 parents who don't use the kind of child care that ABC would subsidize would also lose out. So, too, would private-sector and religious day-care providers. Unlicensed neighborhood day-care providers prove especially vulnerable under ABC because they're very unorganized and because even private-sector day-care centers want to drive them out of business through regulation. Despite the claims that unlicensed neighborhood day care is terrible, in the only available study on unlicensed day care, researchers found it to be of reasonably high quality in comparison to other types of day care.

Recapitulating Deborah Walker's analysis, Rector stressed that a day-care policy based on tax credits can mean either restraint in government spending or it can mean tax increases elsewhere. As a way to curtail the growth of government Rector could not think of a more practical approach than cutting taxes. Admitting that he had never met a tax cut he didn't like, he felt it tactically prudent to push forward on tax reduction wherever one is obtainable. Tax credits for families could be secured within the next five years or so, he predicted. Since families with children are facing significantly higher tax rates than they did 30 years ago, such cuts would be historically justified. In practical, fiscal terms, these families are rearing the taxpayers who will be paying for our social security and other benefits in the future. Rector bristled at the description of a tax cut for families as a measure favoring a "special-interest group." If families are a special-interest group in the same sense that the NEA is a special-interest group, he complained, then the term is becoming too broad to characterize much of anything. By making an investment in the future, families with children carry our culture forward, fulfilling an esteemed social purpose that should be honored in public policy. Rector resisted the notion that children are consumption items morally equivalent to VCR's. It is time, he urged, to recreate the tax haven around child-rearing that existed in the 1950's and early 1960's.

Rector emphasized that the tax-cut policies proposed as an alternative to ABC would assist all low- and moderate-income parents with young children not just those paying for day care.

MacDonald was pleased that Rector had commented on the "progressive mentality" of those who have jumped on board the ABC bandwagon for reasons that are hard to figure out. Recalling Walter Mondale's failed effort to win enactment in the early 1970's for a Federal child care program, he wondered why this movement hasn't succeeded before and why anyone should worry that it is going to this time. The force of ideology, he reminded participants, had been around for some time during a period when many women were going into the labor market. Perhaps, he supposed, it had taken some time for people to see that day care is in their own interest and to organize politically.

Without relying on the rigor of any public-choice model for predicting political outcomes, Deborah Walker predicted that ABC would not pass.

James Walker noted that while it was possible to identify winners and losers for any piece of legislation, timing determines victory or defeat.

War provided a metaphor for Rector, who asked, "Why do you have a major push on a particular section of the front at a given time?" He interpreted recent events in light of a document developed by the Democratic National Committee as a part of their '88 campaign strategy. This document stated that Democrats were suffering politically because the Right had captured symbolic control over family issues. This document outlined a clever strategy for addressing family concerns, so advancing the Democratic cause and splitting the Republican Party in two over its failure to reconcile itself to the "modern family." Rector acknowledged the schizophrenia in Republican thinking on family issues, seeing an illustration in the fragmented Republican response to the ABC Bill. Republicans could not even agree among themselves whether consideration of the traditional family should be incorporated into child-care policy. Meanwhile advocates of a Federal day-care program were planning as early as December of 1987 for a 6- to 8-month media campaign on "the day-care crisis." "It was not an accident," Rector remarked, "that all of a sudden the day-care crisis went from nothing to absolutely saturation coverage during the spring and early summer of the presidential-election year." Rector underscored the working relationship between advocacy groups and the media as decisive in determining which issue is advanced at any given time.

Frank Buchta (an observer at the consultation from The Heartland Institute) asked about the effects on day-care policy of the Civil Rights Restoration Act of 1988 (popularly known as the "Grove City" Bill).

Rector responded that the effects depend on whether the day-care benefit is received as a grant, voucher, or cash. Since the Bush plan would pay cash, the Grove City Bill would not apply to its benefits. On the other hand, the Grove City Bill would govern the distribution of benefits under ABC. More broadly, Rector reiterated, the regulations proposed as part of ABC, would tend to drive out of day care those providers who offer low-cost service. Despite their staunch opposition to ABC, for-profit day-care centers do want to drive these low-cost informal providers out of business by expanding government regulation.

Returning to the question of why the push for public subsidy for day care has come now and not before, Carlson stressed that the whole debate would be academic were it not for Richard Nixon's veto in 1971 of the Mondale-Brademas child care bill. Given the level of pressure on Nixon to sign the measure, Carlson judged his veto "courageous." Carlson felt sure that if it had not been for that veto, the United States would now have a day-care system costing $100 billion a year, with the required participation of all preschoolers. But after Nixon's 1971 veto was sustained by Congress, the day-care issue faded away.

The day-care issue, Rector explained, can only be raised to public consciousness through a tremendous commitment of groups such as the Children's Defense Fund, the Childcare Action League, the National Education Association, and other groups willing to pour incredible amounts of money into the campaign. During the spring of 1988, Rector reported the crusade had waxed so frenetic that even the media began to complain of overkill.

MacDonald's own perception was that the media campaign for day care had actually grown more intense since the Presidential election, a pattern he found strange. He wondered whether anyone supposed that Bush might actually sign the ABC Bill or that his veto might be overridden on the measure.

Rector confidently predicted that Bush would veto a "pure" ABC Bill. But the President would have little impact on any policy that passes Congress unless he makes clear that he will use his veto power regularly until he secures a significant measure of what he wants.

Kohler saw the minimum wage bill as evidence that Congress would sustain the President's vetoes.

On the other hand, Rector thought it unlikely that any of the tax-credit bills (including the one favored by Bush) would ever reach the floor of the House of Representatives for a vote. Compared to the ABC Bill, the tax-credits—which provide much more tangible benefits—are likely to be much more popular with the public at large, making it hard for a congressman to justify an opposing vote.

While tax credits still defined the topic, Kohler took exception to James Walker's focus on the measure as a benefit for parents using institutional day care. Actually, all poor parents of preschoolers would benefit from the Bush tax-credit proposal. Under this plan, even parents who pay few taxes would receive money. In contrast, the ABC Bill would primarily help middle- and upper-class parents, not the less affluent parents who cannot afford the center-based care favored by ABC.

James Walker defended his characterization of the ABC Bill, saying that day care had been defined as an issue because congressmen felt pressure from their constituents, including working women, economically pinched families, and organizations such as the PTA and NEA.

Washington does not respond to constituents, Rector objected. An autonomous entity unto itself, Washington is largely driven by the ideological vision of the Washington establishment. Rector found it inconceivable that the parents of America would unite and march down Pennsylvania Avenue for a day-care bill that would exclude nine out of ten children from any form of assistance. There simply was no constituent pressure for this type of bill. Rather, the sponsors of ABC were motivated by an ideological vision of society requiring day-care centers to complete the liberation of mothers.

James Walker could not square this analysis with Rector's earlier complaint that congressmen evince a *Parade*-magazine mentality. Why should ideologues care what appears in *Parade* magazine?

Rector conceded the need to distinguish between key lobbying groups, unaffected by constituents, and congressmen who do try to interpret constituent needs through the filter of the popular press. Rector recalled that perceptions on day care have been so distorted that in 1988 he found it almost like spitting into a hurricane to testify before Congress that there was no day-care crisis, nor a shortage of day care. Belatedly, now even The Urban Institute has issued a report finding no shortage of day care. The economic data on day care show that the market is working quite well: for-profit centers such as Kindercare and Gerbers operate with average vacancy rates of 25 percent. Still, *Parade* magazine persists in its illusory reports of a chronic shortage of day care.

Why, wondered Chapman, does the press respond the way it does to the interest groups promoting day care?

Rector explained that because of the ideological bias documented by Robert Lichter and Stanley Rothman, the Children's Defense Fund will find it much easier to plant stories than, say, the Cato Institute. In fact, he stated, *Newsweek, The Washington Post,* and *The New York Times* actually contribute funding to the Children's Defense Fund.

How, asked Carlson, do public-choice analysts account for ideology? Behind every ideologue is there an economic interest seeking to assert itself?

Public-choice theorists split on this question, according to Deborah Walker. Robert Tollison would say that economics trumps ideology, while James Buchanan would probably disagree. Although siding with Buchanan on the importance of ideology, Walker believed that a typical politician would sometimes compromise ideology simply to sell proposals.

Economists, Chapman suggested, might regard ideology as comparable to tastes. Deborah Walker agreed.

Redirecting attention away from theory, Kohler ventured that the recent spate of criticism of public education has dampened public desire to place children in day care. At the same time that Americans are learning that the public schools are not very good, day-care advocates are asking them to put more preschoolers in similar circumstances.

Rector complained that according to the peculiar logic of Washington, the failure of the public schools simply means that educators need to start working on the children earlier.

MacDonald credited Kohler with a genuine insight, though, in her belief that the failure of the public schools will foster doubts about day care. He recalled challenging a representative of the public schools who had spoken at a conference on family issues, advocating schooling for younger children at the same time that he catalogued the many serious problems the schools now face. Many heads had nodded in agreement when MacDonald had asked the speaker about the dubiousness of bringing younger children into a system already struggling to cope with older students. People can put 2 and 2 together, MacDonald concluded.

In a flight of fantasy, Vedder wondered how the debate on child care might be different if Ronald Reagan were still President. Perhaps because Bush is viewed as less strong and more pragmatic, proponents of day care hope to negotiate with him. Reagan, on the other hand, might have just repudiated the whole notion.

Back at square one, James Walker wanted to know why day-care policy, of any sort—including tax credits—was desirable or even under debate. What is the constituency? he asked.

But then day care was not *supposed* to be an issue in 1989, Carlson remarked. The proponents of the ABC Bill had supposed that they would have had their way in 1988.

Those advocates could not imagine an alternative. Indeed, at first there wasn't one, except to do nothing, not a popular notion. But once the idea of tax-credits for preschoolers gained life as a viable alternative, it slowed down the day-care movement.

Since two-earner households already receive a tax credit for child care, MacDonald saw the Bush proposal as an attempt to redress an existing bias against maternal child care.

For Rector, tax credits for preschoolers were part of a strategy for taking the policy initiative away from liberals and Democrats. When the day-care issue emerged, conservatives and Republicans were faced with two alternatives. On the one hand, they could acknowledge the existence of a day-care crisis and then propose to spend less money on it than their political adversaries. "That," Rector tartly remarked, "is what we call traditional dime-store Republicanism. It is incredibly boring and it assures . . . permanent minority status." On the other hand, conservatives and Republicans could redefine the issue by asserting that the family is suffering because the state is too large and is taking too much of the family's income. The question is one of marketing ideas. In truth, those pushing for the ABC Bill were trying to do more than win passage for that specific measure: they were marketing the notion that the key to helping families and children is a larger state. If they could once sell that notion, they could depict conservatives as stingy toward children. Conservatives could counter this strategy by urging that families, especially families with young children, deserve tax relief.

Addressing another aspect of the campaign for day care, James Walker challenged the assumption that the average quality of day care would increase if government regulations were enacted. Although empirical research on unlicensed day care is quite scanty, there is no reason to suppose that government regulation would improve the situation. Market mechanisms already exist to maintain the quality of day care. It is a mistake to suppose that regulations are enacted to protect consumers. Rather, the proponents of ABC espouse a very paternalistic philosophy of government, premised upon a distrust of what parents might do with money given them directly. The architects of this plan wish to compel parents to accept only a particular kind of service. Regulation exists not for the consumer, but for the producer, who regards it as a cost of business which will drive out the low-cost producer.

Carlson underscored the importance of power to advocates of the ABC Bill. He recalled attending a public-policy conference at Michigan where he was the only one voicing concerns about day care. For other participants, the conference was almost a religious revival in favor of ABC. The mood reminded Carlson of a scene in *Cabaret* in which a young Nazi boy sings "Tomorrow belongs to me." Speaking of the other participants at the conference, Carlson remarked that "there was this sense that it was going to be their world; the future, history was moving in their direction." To clarify the significance of this sense of power, this arrogance, he recounted his dissertation research on Gunnar Myrdal, who had discovered that many Swedish people were living in bad housing not because they lacked money, but because they were making bad choices. Myrdal therefore concluded that the choices could not continue and that the state must socialize housing to compel people into proper housing. "That mentality," Carlson summed up, "is the whole basis behind a welfare state . . . the presumption that the expert knows best."

On the question of paternalism, Rector detected a total ideological inversion over the last decade, so that conservative welfare policies now focus on ways to give poor people power over their own lives while liberal policies depend on obligatory social services that poor people may not want. For instance, while liberals defend the monopoly control of public-housing authorities, conservatives propose vouchers to give the poor a housing choice in the market. Liberalism begins to represent the interests of the social-services industry, not those of poor people. Only the politics of self-interest explains why advocates of the ABC Bill complain that parents who receive a special tax credit might not spend it on day care. In fact, many poor families do have an infinite number of higher priorities than day care on their minds. Because advocates of day care would rather not acknowledge such preferences, they constantly ignore the traditional one-income families with incomes between $15,000 and $20,000. Not only would this group of families not receive any assistance under ABC, but they would pay significant taxes, while still supporting a family on one income.

An occasional contributor to *Public Choice*, Vedder agreed with Deborah Walker's basic framework for analyzing the day-care debate. The need to enhance job security by attracting votes will largely explain the behavior of politicians who are driven not by ideology but by self-interest. Yet Vedder conceded that the role of ideology in American politics is large and growing. Members of the House of Representatives may be arrogantly following their own preferences and responding less to constituent pressure than in the past because incumbents have rarely lost in recent elections. Vedder found it shocking that job security in the House of Representatives is now greater than in the Supreme Soviet. He wondered whether Congressmen might debate day care differently, if they now faced—as they did 25 years ago—at least an 8 to 10 percent probability of electoral defeat.

A Congressman's job security, in the view of both Kohler and Chapman, actually depends very little upon ideology and a great deal upon how much pork he can deliver to his district. A congressman who effectively defends his district's economic interests, Kohler observed, could vote any way he wanted on an issue such as day care.

In the same vein, Vedder remarked that people consistently complain about Congress as a whole, while idolizing their own Congressman.

Perhaps, conjectured Deborah Walker, Congressmen have so much leeway because their constituents are less well informed and more apathetic than in the past.

Chapman took it as obvious that politics would attract people who derive some sort of satisfaction from pursuing their ideology.

Returning to the question of media, Christensen invoked the work of Christopher Lasch, who discusses how since news has become a commodity, those who profit by it try to produce as much as possible. The natural consequence among the media is an unhealthy appetite for novelty and strangeness. In media coverage of day care, this predictably means that reporters will gravitate toward those proposing something new (putting children into the care of experts), not toward those advocating something old (allowing parents to care for their own children).

This line of analysis seemed plausible to Chapman, who saw in "The Day Care Crisis" *The New York Times* equivalent of the notorious tabloid headline: "Headless Corpse in Topless Bar." Explaining that crises are the media's stock in trade, he noted that newsmen could not report that there are plenty of day-care providers and general satisfaction among parents who employ them. On the other hand, if kids are being short-changed and parents are overloaded; then, that's news. "We make our money in telling people that the world is falling apart; we've got to do something about it." The basic journalistic formula, he concluded, prescribes drama and a moral.

Speaking as historian rather than journalist, Carlson traced the use of "crises" to justify state intervention in the family as far back as the 1830's, the era of the first of America's recurrent juvenile delinquency crises. This period marked the beginning of the reform school movement. For the first time in the United States, experts determined that because parents—especially urban and Irish parents—were doing an inadequate job of raising their children, these children would have to be taken from them and placed in reform schools. So originated the concept of *parens patriae*, the parenthood of the state, born in a decision of the Pennsylvania Supreme Court in 1839 and since constituting a recurring theme of constitutional law defining the parenthood of the state as superior to natural parenthood. Crises occur not simply to satisfy media appetite but to serve an ideology that usually justifies the growth of the state, especially against parental authority. As another instance, Carlson cited the child-labor crisis of the 1920's. While almost everyone now endorses the laws against child labor, the actual debates over the issue were quite fascinating. Even today it is debatable whether a young adult is learning more useful things attending a typical junior high school in Chicago than working in a factory.

But from a different perspective, James Walker saw the push toward day care as part of a plan for reducing government paternalism. Even if the new laws are not enforced, he said, recent welfare reform specifies that any mother with children over three must work, receive education, or begin training. This welfare-reform package—which would require child care—depends on the American faith in self-help, not European belief in universal benefits.

Rector credited Walker with articulating the mythology of the welfare reform. The welfare reform, he insisted, has been deceptively packaged, creating the impression of a work requirement for mothers of children over three but in fact imposing no such requirement. Meanwhile, the rubric of "welfare reform" justified the construction of day-care centers open to families with incomes up to $45,000 per year. Rector especially indicted Senator "Pat" Moynihan for misrepresenting the welfare- reform package, with the help of pliant media.

Rector's analysis smacked too much of conspiracy theory for James Walker, who found it unlikely that there would be no competing media, no conservative press, to expose this kind of fraud. Surely, he urged, there are still rewards for journalists who do investigate work and expose conspiracy.

On the contrary, Rector responded, the rule is now a sort of "pack journalism," so that when a dozen or more reporters say that a bill requires such-and-so, the actual facts may become irrelevant.

Buchta entered the fray to support Rector, reporting that in a recent speech Warren Brooks had complained that the media in Washington usually avoid investigative reporting for fear of being subsequently frozen out of government agencies.

Craven Republicans also deserve blame, Rector added. One Republican in the House of Representatives—Hank Brown—dared to ask, Why don't we actually change things instead of saying we are going to change things? Brown's challenge did generate enough friction to warrant some media coverage. But this media coverage fizzled because Senate Republicans were more interested in supporting a symbolic solution to the welfare crisis than in attacking Senator Moynihan's dishonesty.

On issues such as this one, Vedder believed that only the *Washington Post* and *New York Times* exerted much influence on people in Washington.

To clarify how ideology has affected the day-care debate, Rector redirected attention to the American Civil Liberties Union, a very important influence from the left on this issue. The ACLU has objected to the ABC Bill because it allows money to go to churches, even if the child care provided is thoroughly secular. Because of ACLU pressure, an early version of the ABC Bill required any icons or pictures in a room used for day care to be covered up. For Rector, such egregious provisions illustrate the Talmudic reasoning which guides the ACLU on church-state questions. He thought it too much to hope for that the ACLU would recognize the rational way to separate church from state would be simply to give money to parents and let them spend it as they wish. Rector detected an implicit social as well as an antireligious bias in the opposition to church-based day care. Many on the left find it repugnant that tax money would fund day-care centers run by red-neck Baptist hicks, followers of Jerry Falwell.

Examining the motives of another group prominent in the day-care debate, Carlson pointed out that labor unions have a considerable stake in the issue because fewer Americans work in industry than in the past, while many more provide services. The service sector of the economy appears to define the future for the labor unions.

Changing patterns of work at home puzzled MacDonald. He noted research showing that men have only minimally adjusted their housework to compensate for their wives' employment, leaving many women unhappy. The typical family is now unnecessarily committed to the labor market, he argued, lending his support to a tax policy that would let people keep more of whatever they earn. Such a policy would relieve the financial pressures on parents, making it easier for parents to spend time with their children, especially during tough periods in a child's life. MacDonald was convinced that the family suffers economically because it is less well organized than constituencies that generate forces for taxation.

In the final minutes of the consultation, Rector took aim at prevalent myths about day care. He exploded the notion that families who use day care do so out of economic necessity while only in families with the financial luxury of choice do mothers care for their own children. Over 80 percent of all children in nonparental care come from two-earner households. But the average husband's income in such households is roughly the same as the average husband's income in traditional one-earner households. Overall, families start from similar economic circumstances in making decisions about non-parental care. One group of families chooses a higher income; another group of families makes a financial sacrifice so that they can care for their own children. Washington ignores this pattern as much as possible.

Conventional thinking about the left-right polarity might need revision because of the day-care debate, Rector proposed. He found it intriguing that as a conservative he could now favorably quote from Betty Friedan, who in her book *The Second Stage* calls for economic measures enabling parents to stay home to care for their own children. Of course, he conceded, Friedan's statist outlook prevents her from endorsing tax cuts for families. Yet he thought such tax cuts should appeal to anyone serious about her objectives. Likewise, Rector identified an unusual political evolution evident among the left-wing and liberal mothers active in the group Mothers at Home. Such mothers participated in a recent tax-reduction rally that included a baby-buggy brigade. On the other side of this peculiar realignment, Rector saw day-care advocates trying to forge an unholy alliance with business. Advocates of ABC have tried to win over business groups by arguing that they can keep wages down in the labor-scarce 1990's only if they can bring more mothers of infants into the workforce, while their children go into tax-subsidized day-care centers. For ostensibly left-wing groups to use this line of logic constituted extraordinary hypocrisy, even for Washington, Rector observed.

For Carlson, the new coalition of feminist and business leaders constituted a return to the ideological linkage visible in the past. "Back in the 1920's," he remarked, "the National Association of Manufacturers and the National Women's Party were literally in bed together to get women into the labor force." The feminists of the time wanted emancipation for women; the manufacturers wanted to keep wages low.

MacDonald drew parallels between the current debate over day care and the debate over minimum-wage legislation. It is, he pointed out, hard to defend the minimum wage as an effective or well-targeted benefit for the poor. Yet it has become a totem among people who might be supposed to be economically sophisticated. Over time, ideological rigidity sets in, defining the minimum wage as a measure opposed only by selfish people.

To clarify how American business is responding to the day-care issue, Kohler differentiated between big business and the rest of the business community. While big business is willing, to some extent, to enhance its public image by supporting day care, the rest of the business world has not endorsed day care.

But the U.S. Chamber of Commerce did endorse Senator Orrin Hatch's day-care bill, Rector objected. Perhaps the Chamber's endorsement springs from innate cowardice, he suggested. Rector dismissed the Hatch Bill as "a mini-ABC Bill," a quintessentially Republican gesture: "By gosh . . . there is a crisis, and we intend to spend less money on it."

Reverting to his attack on the ABC Bill, Rector added the Southern states to the list of losers under that bill. Southern states have more formal day care than other states. Because they have more lenient regulation which allows centers to operate at lower costs, ABC regulations would drive up costs enormously in the South, putting many centers out of business. More broadly, Rector was astonished that Washington was willing to move forward on ABC without any understanding of its enormous economic repercussions. When he had challenged advocates of ABC in Congress, they could not produce a single sentence analyzing the impact of their proposed regulations on the cost or supply of day care. At one point, Senator Dodd even argued that raising day-care regulations would reduce costs and expand supply. "Magic- carpet economics" flourishes in Washington, Rector lamented.

In closing, Christensen commented that in the economics of day care, we may see "the shadows of nonrational commitments," utopian, religious, and moral. Satisfied that the day's proceedings had clarified the significance of those shadows, he adjourned the consultation.

Day Care Index—
Names and Topics